Get Ready!
Get Called!
Go!

Get Ready!
Get Called!
Go!

George D. Durrant

Bookcraft
Salt Lake City, Utah

Library of Congress Catalog Card Number: 78-74966
ISBN O-88494-363-1

First Printing, 1979

Lithographed in the United States of America
PUBLISHERS PRESS
Salt Lake City, Utah

To my son Matt
who helped me write this book

CONTENTS

INTRODUCTION

To all young pre-mission men, undecided young women, and uncertain older couples

Dear Friends:

This is not a "fact" book but a "feeling" book. If you like "facts," then read on anyway. It'll do you good. And if you like "feelings," then I have a feeling you'll feel good as you read on.

The primary target of this message is for you young men. Sisters and couples, you are a secondary target, so read on and we'll get to you a little later.

You, my young friend, and I are not exactly alike. Some examples of our differences are as follows: You, while in school, may be a more intelligent student than I was; you may be more athletic than I was; you may be more popular than I was; on the other hand, I was probably more handsome than you are.

Besides being different in talent and in physical attributes, your life situation probably would be different than mine. You might have been raised as a beekeeper's son — I spent my boyhood on a chicken farm. You might have played in the band or run the mile — I wasn't musical or fast. You might have had several "one and only" girl friends — I only had one, and she didn't even know it. You may have been raised in a small town — on the other hand, I was raised in American Fork. You may have been student body president — I was just a student body.

No, we are not exact duplicates of one another. But are we really as different from each other as we are alike?

Consider this story and then we'll look at the question again.

I recall a five-year-old Indian boy whom I knew in Brigham City. He had danced the eagle dance in the Peach Days parade and had delighted each of the thousands who watched from the roadside.

He lived in an apartment near the center of Brigham City, and he didn't even have a dog. (I shouldn't put such sad things in a book.)

While the boy was visiting an uncle in Perry, a small town south of Brigham City, a man recognized him as the boy who had danced in the parade. The man asked, "Would you dance for me?"

The boy replied, "No."

The man said, "Come and see what I've got behind my house."

The boy followed and saw a mother dog and three tiny puppies. The man said, "If you'll dance for me, I'll give you something." And as he said this, he looked at the dogs. The boy looked at the dogs and then at the man. The boy and the man understood each other.

Did the boy dance? (You have five seconds to answer.) Of course he did. You would have too. Any boy would have. How do we know? Because we were once five years old and we know how he felt. What was he thinking while he danced? We know what he was thinking. We don't have to be a psychologist to know. He was thinking, "Which puppy will be mine?"

The boy danced as he had never danced before, and when he finished the man clapped and said: "Because you danced so well, the mother dog and all three of these puppies are yours. Take them home." The boy felt unsurpassed joy.

An hour or so later he and the four dogs arrived at the family's apartment. The mother came to the door. She saw the dogs. She heard the story. And she thought . . . What did she think? How did she feel? Go ask your mother how she felt. She'll know.

Yes, you and I are different all right. But I believe, and you may not care to admit it, that you and I are also very much alike.

Our feelings, though tempered by experience and tampered with by our different environments, are still, when reduced to the most heartfelt level, the same.

True, we have learned to handle our feelings in different ways, and we often hide our emotions from others, but deep down we feel basically the same. You may hear a different drum beat than I hear but we both hear the same drum.

The message of this book will be based on the sameness of our feelings rather than on the differences of our appearance or past experiences. On the pages which follow I have recorded my feelings (which will probably be much like your feelings) about a thrilling word, a word which when heard spans a multitude of our deepest emotions. This word describes an experience which is at first looked forward to, then for two years surrounds our very being and encompasses our total time and talent, and then becomes a treasured and eternal memory. This word is the mighty word *mission*.

A word can be defined in more than one way. For example, the word *house* in a factual way might mean a building with doors, windows, a roof, and walls.

On the pages which follow we will not discuss the word *mission* by describing in any detail what one *does* on a mission but rather what one *feels* while on a mission. The two things are as different as the words *house* and *home*.

In the first three chapters, titled, "Mission?" "Me?" and "Testimony," I will do as I have in the Introduction and shall speak directly to you young men who are approaching missionary age. Feelings about the decision, self-worth, and testimony are discussed.

Chapter four, titled "The Converts," is also addressed to you and will give you the glorious flavor of what it will mean to help in the conversion of a family. Such feelings need to be known as one considers a future mission.

In chapters five and six we leave you, the young man, and focus on the sisters and the couples.

The mission president is the central figure in chapter seven. You'll want to know something about his role and feelings as you plan for your mission.

Then, in the last chapter, "Coming Home," we will focus on you again. But this time it will be a "future" you. You need to know what can be down the road as you consider which path to follow.

And, finally, in the Appendix is a series of newsletters written to missionaries. These will be of interest to you both before and during your mission.

I now invite you to let your feelings be companion to my feelings. (You can even be senior companion if you want.) And let's you and I go forth in our hearts on a mission.

1 / *Mission?*

First, if you haven't read the Introduction, go back and do so. Modesty compels me to say that it's one of the best parts of the book.

I recall many vivid memories of my youthful feelings about someday serving or not serving a mission. My mind flashes back to my senior year at dear old American Fork High School. I can hear again the words of a respected teacher who asked, "George, are you going on a mission?" And my sharp and definite answer, "No, I'm not going on a mission."

Little did I know that just a few years later my bishop would ask, "George, would you accept a call to serve a mission?" And my quick, definite, and emotional answer would be, "Bishop, I'd give my right arm to go."

The decision each of you young men in the Church must make as to whether or not to go on a mission is among the two or three most important decisions of your life. It's a pressurized decision, because in most cases your parents and Church leaders encourage you to go. If you have a girl friend, she may or may not encourage you to go, depending upon the spiritual barometer of her soul. But if she is truly "the right one," she too will say, "Go." She may cry while she says it, but she will still say it. Your friends, if they are active in spiritual matters, will also encourage you to go.

But, on the other hand, you may personally feel that you don't want to go. You might feel that you could never knock on doors, speak on street corners, teach gospel discussions, and in general come face to face with the public. You may feel that your goals and opportunities cannot be abandoned for as long as two years. You might be of the heartfelt opinion that no one has ever been so in love as you and she are. "And perhaps," you say to yourself, "she won't wait. And if I ever lose her I could not go on living."

You might feel that you could never learn the missionary discussions, the scriptures, and especially another language. You may not be a good reader or a good student. You might not consider yourself to be the missionary type. And to yourself you say, "The one thing I don't want to be is a returned missionary." And last of all, you may not have a spiritual conviction that you should go because you don't really have that which is described as a testimony.

Yes, for some young men there are many emotional factors which can be, and so often are, a vital part of the decision about a mission. For some the decision is easy. You may be one who has saved money for, studied for, dreamed of, planned on, and longed for the time when you would be of the age to go. There are many who knew in their boyhood that the Church was true and they have known this throughout all of their years. It is a blessing to be one of these. If you are, there is little likelihood that any influence could keep you from your mission.

But there are those, and you may be one, who have never had a deep conviction of the truth. You may have believed while a child, but through the years you have come to doubt or at least to not really know. For you the decision could be a struggle.

I mention all of these things because to me they are very real. I recall my own feelings. I was the youngest of nine children. Two of my five brothers went on missions and three didn't. My mother was actively involved in Church programs and my father wasn't. So far as allegiance to the Church was concerned, the family was divided down the middle. And I was likewise divided.

Part of me said *go* and part of me said *no*. And the part that said *no* was dominant in my senior year of high school. There were reasons for that. In high school I wanted to be tough. I don't mean get-in-fights kind of tough. I considered that dangerous. But I mean the kind of tough where sentimental movies and stories were to be laughed off rather than cried about. Regular church attendance was desirable but hard to explain to those who felt such things were a bit sissified.

I had an intense desire to be one of the boys — to dress the way tough guys dressed, to comb my hair in the lastest duck tail style, and to have that tough kind of attitude. And returned missionaries didn't meet all of these standards. Don't get me wrong. I wasn't a bad guy; it was just that I wasn't a good guy. Yet in my heart I really did want to be a good guy. In other words, I was confused.

That's why when I was a senior in high school I responded as I did to my teacher. As I said before, he asked, "George, are you going on a mission?" And I replied, "No, I'm not going on a mission."

He then said, "Your brother just got back."

I replied with a little hostility in my tone: "That's my brother, that's not me. He lives his life and I live mine."

He said: "You don't have to get upset. I was just wondering."

I knew then, as you might know now, that it sometimes seems that people are sort of meddling in your personal affairs when they ask about your mission intentions. Yet in my day there was much less pressure to go than there is today. Then only a small percentage of the young men did go. So the peer group pressure of going was not great. There was not then any prophetic statement that every worthy young man should go on a mission.

But I still felt pressure because in my heart I felt that I should go. And that is the greatest pressure of all.

Time changes many things. The ages of eighteen, nineteen and even twenty are unusual years. Life begins to look different than it did at fifteen, sixteen, and seventeen. Being out of high school and wondering about the future places a young man on different ground. Attitudes change and often he begins to think less about "How can I please my friends?" and more about "How do I fit in and how can I help others?"

I did some changing in those late-teen years. I still wanted to be tough but I also wanted to be religious. I didn't yet want to be deeply religious, but I did want to be good and to do good.

I was working my way through college in a job which only allowed me to attend sacrament meeting every other week. When I'd arrive at church, my bishop would greet me warmly and ask me to give the closing prayer. After a few weeks of this, I decided that I must be the only one who could give a closing prayer, because it seemed like each time I came I'd be asked to give it. I'd sit in the congregation until the last verse of the closing song, then I'd head for the pulpit. I'd arrive just as the last word was sung. I'd close my eyes (and that helped because I was deeply self-conscious and didn't feel secure with so many people watching me). Then I'd begin to speak. I would experience a closeness to the Lord as I spoke the words which expressed the feelings of my heart. Giving those prayers was a spiritual experience for me. If it hadn't been for those opportunities given to me by a loving bishop, I don't believe I would have ever known the thrill of a mission.

Yet even at that time in my life I didn't want to go. I really feared going. I wondered: "How could I ever do it? I can't even convince a girl to go out with me, how could I ever convince anyone to join the Church?"

Insecurity was my greatest roadblock. That, plus I didn't think I could stand not seeing my mom for two long years.

Two years! That seemed as if it would be forever. And besides, I didn't even know for sure the Church was true. I had had no great spiritual experience nor had I ever sought any. There was also still the desire to be tough and about all that meant now was to not be too religious. And a mission seemed too religious.

At college I began to gain a little more self-confidence. I found I could make people laugh. I worked on developing my sense of humor. I began to realize that being funny was almost as good as being tough. I was also learning to be an artist.

Returned missionaries were plentiful at college. Some of them were funny, some were real ladies' men. I started thinking that they weren't so bad after all. I heard one speak at a fireside. He was quite handsome. The girls laughed at his jokes and looked at him in awe. He nearly cried as he expressed his spiritual conviction about the Church. As I listened, I almost felt jealous. I guess we are always a bit jealous of someone when we wish we were like them.

About that time Elder Matthew Cowley of the Quorum of the Twelve spoke at a devotional at BYU. Listening to his experiences in New Zealand made me laugh. Then he'd say things that made me feel like crying. Because I was too tough, I wasn't going to cry. But I couldn't help it; I cried. When he finished, I surrendered. I had an intense desire to be religious.

It was then that I learned the great secret — when you become religious you don't have to quit being tough. I believe I'm a living example of that because I'm religious and I'm really tough. As a matter of fact, I don't believe you can be religious without being tough. You have to be tough to be religious. And the best catalyst to blend the two is a good wholesome sense of humor.

Not long thereafter I received the Melchizedek Priesthood and was ordained to the office of elder. That did something to me. It gave me self-respect. It caused me to begin to like myself and to be grateful that I was me.

But through all of this I still did not have a testimony. I was thrilled to be an elder and to serve the Lord, but I had received no spiritual witness that the Church was true.

Then came the phone call: "George, this is Bishop Grant. Could you come to my house? I need to talk to you." Fifteen minutes later came the most glorious of all queries, "George, would you accept a call to serve a mission?"

With all my heart I responded, "Bishop, I would give my right arm to go."

The paper work began and with it those glorious days of waiting for the unknown place, and the unimaginable adventure which is encompassed in the word *mission.*

I realize that the road I have just described which led me to my mission isn't exactly like the road which you now tread. Here is an example of another road. I recall a fellow in a class which I taught at BYU. He was a young spiritual giant. I would call upon him to respond in class and his answers were filled with both substance and conviction.

He always sat close to a beautiful young girl who seemed to adore him. Unbeknown to me, they were planning marriage within the year.

I was somewhat shocked when I learned that he had not yet served a mission. He seemed to have the maturity and insight of someone who had so served. I also learned that he was a freshman. I had thought him to be older.

I became enthusiastic about his future and, not knowing about his matrimonial plans, I inquired as to when he would be leaving for his mission.

His quick and seemingly well-rehearsed answer was: "Oh, I'm not going. I feel that isn't a necessary part of my life at this time." He added that later in life he and she would serve a mission together.

I learned that much parental pressure had been exerted to get him to change his mind. But so far this pressure seemed to only drive him deeper into his determination not to go.

Friends and Church leaders also endlessly suggested that he go. But he would not budge. His girl friend had learned of his determination not to go and she, knowing of his goodness, decided that she would abandon her own desire for him to serve and would go along with his wishes.

I realized the pressure he had already faced and withstood. I was determined not to add my voice to that seemingly futile force. But I could not help saying to him, "There is something I'll never know and I'll wonder about it for a long time."

He asked, "What's that?"

I replied, "I keep wondering if you would have been as great a missionary as I think you could be."

He smiled and asked, "What do you mean?"

I said: "I keep remembering when I was mission president. I can just see me waiting at the airport. The plane lands and you walk down the ramp toward me." I paused, looked deep into his eyes, and added: "I used to pray long prayers that the Lord would send me missionaries such as you. Oh! my friend you would have been a great one. But anyway it doesn't matter because you aren't going."

"Why would I have been a great one?" he asked, seeming to fish for a compliment.

I was more than willing to sincerely take the bait and I responded: "You would have been a great one because of the way you walk and talk and smile. The way leadership is part of your very bearing. Your knowledge, your smile, your love. What I could do as a mission president if I had you!" I then felt myself near tears as I concluded by shaking my head and exclaiming, "What a waste!"

He had no answer. I sensed he was pained, so I continued: "I don't want to add to your pressures. God bless you in your plans." I had no desire to manipulate him but I couldn't be anything less than sincere, and that is why I had said what I did.

A few days later he and his girl friend were in my office. He spoke: "I just can't go. We have our marriage planned." He paused and looked at her. Tears came into her eyes as he said: "What do you think? What if I went? Would you wait?"

She cried openly and could not speak for a time. Then amidst her tears she said, "If you go, I'll wait."

"But do you want me to go?"

"I want you to go if you want to. But I wish so much that you would want to."

They left, having made no firm decision. A day later they returned. He asked, "If I went, do you feel it would be to a Spanish-speaking mission?" I answered as best I could. But there was still no decision.

A week later they entered my office with radiant smiles and he announced: "My papers are in. I hope it's Spanish, but wherever it is will be all right." A few weeks later he walked down an airline ramp to meet a mission president who had been praying for someone like him. I think that she will wait, don't you? Some do, you know.

I've told you my pre-mission story and that of my student friend. I'd love to hear your story. After all, your story is the only one that really matters. I'm praying for you. You'd be a great one because you are you.

2/ *Me?*

The jetliner lands and taxis to the concourse. The door opens and out come the passengers. Almost three-fourths of the travelers are out now, but still the missionaries aren't in sight.

Suddenly the mission secretary shouts, "There they come," as four of them head down the ramp together. One more is close behind. Then come ten more passengers. Another two young Elders follow them. Finally, after all others are out, a count is taken. There is a feeling that one Elder must have missed the plane. But then a few seconds later he appears in the doorway of the airplane and hurries along to catch up.

So all eight of the tall, short, thin, husky group have officially arrived in the mission field.

The president stands waiting to greet his new arrivals. He shakes hands with each one and greets each by name. He's memorized the names and the faces by using the photos which they mailed to him some days before.

The first Elder to greet the president has hurried ahead so that he could be the first. He is determined to get off to a good start. He waited a long time for his mission and now that it's finally here he wants to be first in everything. He left no girl behind because he felt that would not be good for him as a missionary. He's not too tall and is slightly built. He wasn't on any school teams, but he loves sports. He was not a student body officer, but he took part in school plays.

The second Elder to be greeted is six feet four inches tall and is very slight of frame. He comes from a farm in northern Utah. He doesn't say anything to the president, but grins widely and after shaking hands quickly stands aside to let others shake hands. He didn't participate in athletics because he had to get home from school each night to help with the work on the dairy farm. He hasn't slept in past 5:00 A.M. in the last seven years.

The third Elder is limping as he approaches. He was injured in an auto accident at age fourteen. He is rather shy. As he shakes hands, he looks away from the president's eyes.

The fourth Elder to be greeted says with exuberance: "Well, President, here I am. I hope you haven't baptized everybody out here yet because I need at least a thousand converts to meet my goal."

The president reponds, "Oh, we've got a thousand waiting for you."

The Elder, a former guitar player in a dance group and also a radio disc jockey, replies, "But you must understand, President, that it will take me a week or so to do that." Everyone laughs.

The fifth Elder is short and husky. The president says, "And you must be the national high school wrestling champion." The Elder seems embarrassed and replies, "Yeah, I guess so."

The sixth Elder is quite small. He has been sick on the airplane and still looks a bit shaky. He has been a poor student and isn't able to read very well. As of late he's found the world of girls. He has left some twelve girl friends behind.

The seventh Elder is about six feet tall. He has blond hair. He is a national merit scholar. He greets the president warmly and says: "Brother Simmons says he knows you. He told me to tell you hello."

"Oh, yes," says the president, "how is Jim?"

"He's fine," replies the Elder. "He told me I was coming to the best president in the world."

The eighth Elder says: "I'm sorry I was a little late, but I went back to get the bag of peanuts they gave me. I asked the stewardess if she could help me find them. She wanted to know who we all were. I gave her a Book of Mormon. She was really cute. I bet she'll join the Church."

The missionaries, the president, the mission secretary and the two assistants walk to the baggage claim area. Five of the new arrivals are talking to the mission secretary. One says: "We were talking on the way out here and we were wondering when the mission actually starts. Did it start when we went into the missionary training center or does it start after we arrive here?"

Another Elder says, "It starts when we go in the missionary training center, doesn't it?"

Another said: "It starts today. We got here today so that's when it starts."

The secretary speaks: "Okay, I'll settle this for you. Everybody look at your watches." The secretary lifts his right hand as he looks at the second hand on his watch. When it has swept its way up to twelve, he brings his right hand down. As he does, he says with enthusiasm: "Your mission starts now. Go!"

The new Elders look at him in amazement. The assistants laugh and the luggage arrives.

So, eight new Elders have just started their missions. They all started at "go." What will their stories be? Will each be successful? What background does it take to qualify one to be a good missionary?

Will the enthusiasm of the first Elder who wants to be first cause him to be first?

Will the early-rising, hard-working, silently smiling farm boy lead the mission in hours worked?

Will the Elder with a physical impairment be able to keep up with the rigorous pace of missionary work?

Will the sense of humor of the thousand-a-week missionary get in the way of the serious spirituality needed by a missionary?

Will the dedication of the national champion wrestler transfer over into the discipline needed to be a truly great missionary?

Will the small Elder with a nervous stomach and a reading problem be able to take the pressure of learning the discussions?

Will the merit scholar be able to use his intellectual gifts to engage in successful Bible bashes with the Bible-studying Baptist minister?

Will the Elder who forgot his peanuts be able to take care of the many details of missionary work which are even more important than peanuts?

If you were a betting man, which of these eight Elders would you put your money on? Which one will be the most successful?

Don't be too quick to judge. We haven't got enough evidence. Someday the mission secretary will be able to say to these eight: "Your full-time mission ends now! Go home!" And then we'll know which of the eight had what it takes to be successful.

I learned as a mission president that it was difficult to tell when missionaries arrived just which ones would really blossom into full-blown missionaries.

I've always sort of worshipped athletes. A good athlete should make a good missionary. But some struggle because the crowd isn't there to play to. And if they have come to feel that all else revolves around them, they sputter as missionaries. But if they are team players who have attributed their success to the Lord, they are on the threshold of greatness.

The hard-working farmer has the main ingredient. He'll do well if he can couple the Spirit with his work.

Student body leaders have the personality to influence people. If they are sincere and willing to follow as well as lead, they can do well.

But what of those who have not led the world, or the town, or the ward, or the family in anything? Those who can't speak in Church, who are frightened to teach a class, who don't really like to meet new people or face new challenges. What about those who either dropped out of school or at least wanted to? Those who would sooner work on cars or drive trucks than they would read, write, or do math. Can they succeed?

With all my heart I want to shout that they can be the very backbone of the work. These noble men who struggle, if they become partners with God, can be the truly great ones.

A mission is a new beginning. Basically all that one has accomplished is left behind. Of course, talents can't be left behind, but opportunity to develop talents lies before the newly arrived missionary like an open football field where all opposing players have been knocked down. All that is needed is a steady, sincere, two-year romp to the goal line.

In high school I was a "dud." I didn't want to be but I was. I wanted to be student body president, but I didn't get elected because I wasn't nominated. I wasn't nominated because no one thought I'd be a good president. I was the only one who knew, and I didn't mention it because I thought everyone would laugh.

I wasn't all-state because it's hard to make all-state while sitting on the bench. If a sports writer would look over at me, I'd sit up straight, but still they wouldn't name me all-state.

So when I arrived in England on my mission, I wasn't exactly Mr. World.

But the great thing about it was that the people in England didn't know that I was a dud. They saw me in my nice navy blue suit and they thought I was a great Elder. And for two years I wore that navy blue suit. And the people kept thinking I was great. (They thought all of us were.)

I recall the day after we arrived we received an orientation from our president. Then each of the eight of us was asked to give a little report out of a book on missionary work. I was doing mine when I saw the president look at his assistant and nod his head up and down in approval. I could hardly go on, I was so excited. That little bit of approval from this great man was like being listed as a starter in the state tournament.

The next day my president said, "Elder Durrant, you go to Hull."

I said: "Excuse me, where was that?"

He replied, "Hull — H-U-L-L."

So, I went to Hull.

I quickly picked up the language there in England and started to give it my all. I had so much to learn. Most of the eight I came out with had been student body leaders. Others in the mission possessed many noteworthy attributes. And there I was in the midst of all of them.

I wasn't a speaker, I wasn't a scholar, I wasn't a great athlete. I didn't really even have a testimony. And most of all I was deeply frightened.

I recall that my first prayer in England occurred when the ship was docking. My prayer was prompted by the thought, "Could I possibly swim home?" I prayed, "Oh, dear Father, just give me the strength to go ashore."

And starting with such a humble beginning and with so little to qualify me for the work, I became the greatest average missionary to ever serve in England.

My mission became my everything.

You might say, "That's your story, but what about me?"

To that I'd reply: "If I were still mission president, I'd like you. The Lord wants you. Your parents would like to get rid of you. Your girl friend would get over you in a while (I'm just kidding on that). So come on. Put your hand into the hand of the Lord. You aren't exactly like any of the eight who arrived earlier in this chapter and you aren't exactly like me. That's why you are so sorely needed. There is something to do that needs a man just like you. Certain people are waiting for their missionary to come. And their missionary isn't perfect, because he is you."

3 / *Testimony*

Ideally, one should depart for his mission with a burning testimony of the divine mission of the Church, a conviction that Joseph Smith was a prophet and an inward witness that Jesus Christ is the Son of God and the Savior of the world.

And those who come with such feelings are a light to the entire mission. They can be effective in their missions from the beginning to the end. But for some, much pre-mission spiritual depth is not yet part of them. They want to know, but they don't yet know.

A few minutes after I had said to my bishop, "I'd give my right arm to go," I was standing in the service station where I worked. I excitedly told my boss, "I'm going on a mission."

He was a little shocked at first, but then he spoke: "I'm glad you are going. It is better than college. It is better than the army. You'll learn so much. When you get home, you'll be more confident. You will be able to meet people better. You'll be able to speak and to lead."

He then jokingly added, "We'll miss you." As he said this, his mood changed and he continued, "There is just one thing I'd like you to promise me."

I asked, "What's that?"

He replied quickly and with a bit of emotion. "When you get home, don't stand up and say that you know the Church is true."

He paused as we looked into each other's eyes. Then he continued: "There is no way you can know that, George. You are honest and so I know that you won't lie. All those who say that they know the Church is true are liars. I don't go to church because of all those who stand up and say that. There is no way that they can know."

He concluded by saying: "George, you'll do great. But remember, you are honest. Don't come home and say that you know the Church is true because neither you nor anyone else can know that."

The joy I had felt with the bishop went out of me and doubt crept in. I didn't really *know* the Church was true. I hoped it was. I did know that prayers were answered and I knew that there was a God, but beyond that I didn't know.

In the days that followed, the excitement carried me along. I was treated in the special way that people treat those who are soon to leave on missions. Then there was a long series of thrills — buying a navy blue suit, being photographed for a missionary picture, having a farewell where girls came that I didn't even know cared, shaking hands until my own hand ached from grasping the hands of hundreds (though it seemed like thousands) of well-wishers.

Then the mission home. (When I went on my mission, we went to the mission home in Salt Lake.) I'll always remember the mission home.

"Tomorrow morning we go to the temple," the mission president said. "You all were told to bring your recommends and so we know you did."

Then it hit me. In all my preparation I'd forgotten to get a recommend. I felt sick. I panicked: I'll probably be sent home before I even leave Utah. How could I be so dumb? I don't dare tell the president.

Shortly thereafter the meeting ended. Others headed for the evening meal. I ran toward downtown Salt Lake City. I've never been more upset. I saw a phone booth. I entered. I'd call my bishop. He'd help. He lived in American Fork, some thirty-five miles away, but he worked for the highway patrol. I'd call the highway patrol. In the Yellow Pages I searched for the number. "Oh, no!" There were at least filfteen different numbers. My finger trembled as it moved from one number to the next. I prayed,"Oh, please, let me call the right place." I decided on a number and dialed it. "Highway patrol," a woman's voice answered.

"I . . . ah was . . . well . . . I'm trying to reach Mel Grant."

"Mel Grant," she said in a surprised voice. "How did you know he was here?" I said I didn't know. She said, "He almost never comes here, but he's here now."

A moment later I was speaking to my bishop. (Bishops are good to have.) I told him of my plight. He said, "I'll go right home, get the recommend, get it to the stake president, and then give it to a patrolman who'll rush it to you."

That night in the evening session a patrolman entered the back of the hall. All eyes were fixed upon him as he made his way to the stand and whispered to the mission president. The president then arose, interrupted the speaker, and stated, "This man desires to see Elder Durrant."

I arose, and as I began to walk to the foyer I felt the stare of each one in the room. A moment later the patrolman gave me my glorious ticket. A ticket to the temple, which for me was the beginning of a testimony. That night my prayers were quite intense. It felt good to know that the Lord took care of one young man who needed help so desperately. And he continued to help me.

But after the excitement of going was over, then came the discouragement of being there. After a month or so in Hull I again began to wonder about trying to swim home. A series of events were disturbing and discouraging.

My bike (sold to me by another Elder) wasn't as good as he said. It was extremely difficult to pedal, and the generator wouldn't generate.

The English fog was so thick.

From home I received word that our ward basketball team had made it to the all-Church tournament — something I'd desired to be part of with all my heart. I couldn't understand how they did it without me. I had been their star!

Word also came that Elder Matthew Cowley, my spiritual hero, had died.

I didn't get any Christmas presents from home.

My landlady, whom I had come to love because she reminded me of my mother, became desperately ill.

I wasn't learning the discussions very fast and had about decided I could never learn so much.

Our investigators weren't too anxious to investigate.

I caught a cold (I only had one cold on my entire mission but it lasted for two years).

Finally, after a month or so it was Christmas day and I cannot ever recall being so depressed. We didn't have Christmas dinner where we lived because of the landlady's illness. And I was too near pneumonia to venture out into the fog to go to a member's house.

Stripped of all the things I had come to associate with Christmas, I was indeed down in the mouth.

I sat looking into the glowing coal embers of a warm fire. Out of the corner of my eye I saw my Bible. Almost subconsciously I reached over and picked it up. Opening it to the book of Matthew, I began to read. My mind gradually shifted away from my troubles and sorrows. I began to focus my thinking on the glorious mission of the Savior. On that Christmas day I walked with him. In my mind I could see him heal the sick, encourage the sinner to repent, criticize the hypocrites, comfort the sorrowful. I saw him walk on the water, and hold the children in his arms. I agonized with him in the garden and watched him die on the cross. I felt a surge of hope as I witnessed him rise from the tomb.

I've never had such a Christmas. I spent it with him.

A few nights later I had a dream about him and about my relationship to him. I don't think I'll ever be the same again because of that dream.

I then knew that he was indeed the Savior of the world. My testimony was firmly forming.

A month or so later my district president asked me to give a talk in a forthcoming missionary meeting on the subject of Joseph Smith.

The other Elders had taken their turns and each had deeply impressed me. I wanted to do as well. I was fearful that I'd forget and not be able to speak with any fluency.

I studied with more intensity than I'd ever done before. I prayed for the ability and courage to speak with clarity and power.

Finally the time arrived. We, nine other Elders and myself, were assembled on the front two rows of the little Hull chapel.

I stood to speak. My fear was soon replaced by other emotions. Something seemed to be happening deep inside my soul. I said, "And in response to Joseph Smith's prayer, God the Father and his Son Jesus Christ appeared to him."

When I said that, I felt a feeling that made me begin to cry. I tried to go on but I could not. I looked down at the floor and I sobbed. Finally, I was able to gain some control. I looked into the faces of my companions. They too were in tears. I was then able to speak again. I told of the persecution and the martyrdom of the Prophet.

I then sat down. But I was not the same person who had stood up, for now I *knew.* I knew that the message I was proclaiming was true. I knew that The Church of Jesus Christ of Latter-day Saints was indeed what its name says — the Lord's church. It is my belief that on that day in England I became a man.

And what I recall from my own experience, I also witnessed many times in the lives of the missionaries with whom I served and others over whom I presided as president.

Let's go back to the eight Elders whom we greeted earlier at the airport. Remember the wrestler? Let's look at him because, although he's a great athlete, he is sort of typical in other ways.

We have driven with the eight Elders from the airport. We are in the mission home. We've just had dinner and are now in the front room having a rather informal meeting.

One by one the president asks each missionary why he came on a mission. One says, "I always wanted to." Another responds, "I'm a convert and I wanted to give others what I have been given."

Finally it is the wrestler's turn. He starts to speak and as he does his eyes focus on the floor just in front of his chair. He stares at that same spot all the while he says: "I don't know why I came. I don't have a testimony or anything like that." He pauses and continues: "I was pretty lucky at wrestling and got all these scholarship offers. I finally went to college. With a few breaks I was able to win the conference in my weight.

"I met this girl in college and I really liked her. We went to the April general conference because she wanted to. We arrived at the Tabernacle at four in the morning and eventually managed to obtain a seat in the balcony.

"The President of the Church was talking about missionary work. He said, 'Every worthy young man ought to go.' We were holding hands and she tightened her grip on me when he said that.

"After the meeting we were sitting on the lawn by the Visitors Center. I had not really planned on a mission. My parents aren't active and they sort of wanted me to keep going to college on my scholarship.

"I asked my girl friend if she felt I ought to go. She replied that she had always wanted to marry a returned missionary. Before I knew what had hit me, I told her I was going."

The Elder now looked up and as he did he said, "President, I don't know why I'm here." Tears caused his eyes to glisten as he said: "I miss her so much. I wish I were home." He didn't speak for a few seconds and the room was filled with perfect silence. Then he drew a deep breath and squared his shoulders and said: "But I'm here and I'm staying. I'll just do my best and see what happens."

Two months later at a zone conference he stands to take his turn in testimony bearing. He speaks: "President, these have been the two hardest months of my life. Wrestling is a breeze compared to this. I've struggled with the scriptures and with the discussions. My companion is a great man, but I'm afraid we get on each other's nerves at times.

"The other night we were teaching a man and his wife. This guy had been drinking and he was sort of making fun of what I was saying. I showed him the Book of Mormon and told him about it. I told him about Joseph Smith. As I spoke, I could tell that he didn't believe what I was saying, but all of a sudden I realized that I believed what I was saying.

"President and Elders and Sisters, I found out that I've got a testimony. And I want to tell all of you that this Church is true. I know that it is. I still miss my girl and at times I still wish I were home. But I'd rather be here doing this work than to be anywhere else doing anything else."

He now had the dimension that would make a great wrestler a great missionary. He came without a testimony but he came with a desire. And a righteous desire mixed with mission experiences always results in a testimony. But it is not always easy.

I remember another Elder who told me, "President, I want to go home."

"But," I replied, "you've only been here six months."

"I know," he answered, "but I can't go around telling people about something that I don't even believe myself."

We had a long talk. I tried to get him to stay, but he felt he was too honest and he didn't want to be a hypocrite.

I asked him to read the Book of Mormon. He said he already had. I asked him to pray about it and he said he had done so thousands of times. I asked him to stay another month and he said he wouldn't.

I asked him what he'd do at home. He said he would probably get married.

I asked, "Won't she be disappointed that you came home early?"

He replied: "No, she understands. I told her and my parents that I'd try it for six months and then decide to stay or come home."

He continued: "So now I've done that. The Lord hasn't told me it's true, as he has all the others, and so I'm going home."

What is the problem in this case? Why hasn't this Elder received a testimony? What could he do that he has not done? He came. He studied. He prayed.

What does he lack?

Could it be commitment?

He is on the verge of everything but is giving up just before he reaches the mark.

He needs to say: "Heavenly Father, I've really tried. But it's hard to continue without a testimony. I'm not going to go home. I committed to you to serve two years, but I need help. Please help me."

And then the trial would be complete and into his soul would come that quite wonderful feeling that indeed the Church is true. Jesus Christ is the Savior. Joseph Smith was a prophet. In striving to gain a testimony we often come to know the truthfulness of Moroni's words wherein he said, "For ye receive no witness until after the trial of your faith." (Ether 12:6.)

One must have a spiritual experience to be a full-powered missionary. The Lord has promised that if we will knock, he will hear and open the door.

I knew another missionary who operated at half-power for six months. He was a fine-looking man. He had personality. But he seemed to have no spiritual depth. His attempt at bearing his testimony was more of a story or two about gratitude and a funny experience with his companion. He was entertaining but spiritually shallow.

In regular interviews he claimed that all was well.

But one day he finally broke down and said, "President, there is something I must tell you." He then tearfully confessed his past errors. His heart was broken and his spirit was contrite.

He had knocked on the door. The channel was clear. Testimony flowed in and with it came full power.

Where one is raised (farm or city, small town or large), what one has done (been prominent or obscure), whether one is handsome or plain, exuberant or quiet makes little difference. Great missionaries are all different kinds of men. But in obedience, positive attitude, love and testimony, and moral cleanliness they are all the same.

These are the things which bring success. Each missionary has an equal chance. It's all a matter of seeking after these things. That's why we couldn't judge the eight missionaries who just arrived in the mission field. Their success depends not upon what they've been, but upon what they are now and, more importantly, upon what they can become.

On a mission one can reach greatness. Especially one like you. And when one comes home, he can say with sureness, "My dear brothers and sisters, I know that Joseph Smith was a prophet, that this is the true Church, and that Jesus Christ is the Savior."

I was able to do that. My boss was there to hear. I know not what he thought, but to have failed to say these things would have made me a liar.

4 / The Converts

SCENE I

Let's go tracting.

I'll be senior companion and you be junior (or if you don't like that, you be junior and I'll be senior).

We are told in the scriptures to be bold and warn our neighbors. Let's try that approach. We'll leave our bikes chained to this utility pole and tract the houses which we feel impressed to call on. Let's go on this side of that street right over there.

I'll take the first door.

Knock, knock.

(A lady comes to the door. She looks a bit angry. Her baby just put his honey-covered hands on her new drapes. Her husband was cross this morning before he went to work. She doesn't have time to talk because she is washing and ironing.)

"Good morning, Ma'am. We are just in the neighborhood boldly warning people. We'd like to warn you."

She replies: "I'm warning you. If you don't leave right now, I'll have the police here."

We leave. We were bold and we warned her, but something was missing.

Let's see, what was it Alma told his son Shiblon about being bold? Oh, yes. He said we should be bold but not overbearing.

Let's try another door, Elder. Let me try one more, and if I don't do better you can take over.

Knock, knock.

"Good morning, Ma'am. I'm Elder Durrant and this is Elder Matthews. I can see you are busy." (Her little boy just pulled the tablecloth off the table and broke three of the breakfast cereal bowls, and her husband was also cross before he left for work.)

"Yes, I am busy," she replied. "I have no time to talk." (She begins to close the door.)

"I was just wondering who planted these petunias?" I ask.

She replies: "I did, but what do you want? I'm busy."

"My mother grows petunias back home. Hers look just like these. I really miss her. I haven't seen her in thirteen months. You see, I left home and came on a mission to tell people about the Lord's true church. But I sure miss my mother."

"I'm sure you do, but I haven't got time to talk about petunias." (She again starts to close the door.)

You, my companion — we'll call you Elder Matthews — see a little boy behind his mother and say: "Hi there, what's your name? He's sure a cute little guy. How many children do you have, Ma'am?"

"Five."

"Five? That's the same as we have. I have a little brother just about his size. How old is he?"

"Three."

"What's his name?"

"Charlie."

"Hi, Charlie. Is that your doggie sleeping over there in the sun?"

"He's sure a fine boy, Ma'am. You see, we are in the neighborhood calling on families. We have a great plan to teach families how to have a good time together. We know you are busy, but could we just come in for a moment?"

"Oh, I'm so busy but I suppose so, just for a minute."

Once inside I say, "Oh, who plays the piano?"

And you add, "Did your husband kill the deer and have the head mounted?"

We are almost in chorus as we say, "This certainly is a lovely home."

We sit down and as we do, I speak: "It looks as if the dog likes us. Go over and get on Elder Matthews' lap. He loves dogs. What's his name?"

"As we were saying, we have a program for families; but before we tell you about it, could we offer a word of prayer in your home?"

"Elder Matthews would you stand and say the prayer?"

(Elder Matthews prays for the family. The lady is touched by his simple, gentle appeal to the Lord on behalf of her family.)

I speak again: "That was a fine prayer, Elder Matthews. What we'd like to do is to call back when your husband is at home. We'll be back in the neighborhood on Wednesday evening about seven. Would your husband be home then?"

"I think so."

"All right, we'll write that down and be back at that time."

"You've got quite a son there, Mrs. Riggs. We'll be anxious to meet Mr. Riggs and the other four children. So long for now."

SCENE II

It's Wednesday night. We chain our bikes to the utility pole and head toward the house.

Inside the house the following is occurring.

Mr. Riggs is speaking. "That was a fine meal. Now for TV. Laying brick all day has about got to me. Could you bring me a cold drink?"

"Sprite?"

"No, not Sprite. You know what I want."

"Oh, by the way, Honey, a couple of young men are coming by in a few minutes."

"Young men? What do they want?"

"To talk about religion, I think."

"Religion! I don't want to talk about religion. I'm tired, and you know I never go to church anyway. If they come, get rid of them."

"But Honey, they are really nice."

"I don't care how nice they are. Get rid of them."

"I'm not going to. If you don't want them to come in, you tell them to leave."

"I'll tell 'em. What are their names?"

"One of them was really handsome, and I think the other one was named Elder Matthews."

"Elder? Are they Mormons?"

"I don't know."

(And about that time), knock, knock, knock.

"I'll get rid of them."

"Hi, Mr. Riggs. Your wife invited us to come by . . ."

"Well, I'm uninviting you. I'm tired and not interested."

"All right, but before we go could we just have one more look at the deer head by the fireplace?"

"What for?"

"Well, we were talking about it. Is it a mule deer?"

"No, it's a white tail."

"Could we see it one more time? Back home we don't have those kind."

"Well, I don't know. I'm watching TV."

"We'd only take a minute."

"Well, come in then."

"Wow, that's a beauty! Did you get him with a rifle?"

"Oh, no, we use shotguns here."

"Shotguns? We use rifles back home."

"Rifles? Don't people get shot?"

"Oh yeah, a few."

"Could we see your gun?"

(He gets his shotgun.)

"This is a beauty. Someday you ought to come out home and I'd take you after a mule deer."

He excitedly answers: "I'd love that. I've read about them in *Field and Stream* magazine."

"While we are here, Mr. Riggs, if you've got a little time, we'd love to just explain why we came."

"Oh, sure. Sit down. Kids, turn off the TV."

"Get away from him, Blacky. Don't get up on his lap."

"That's all right, Mr. Riggs. Elder Matthews loves dogs."

"We'd like to have a word of prayer before we go on."

"Sure, but I'm not really religious."

"That's all right. With your permission I'll say the prayer."

"Kids, be really quiet. The man's going to pray."

(After the prayer I speak again.)

"Now kids, let me teach you a good song. We call this family home evening, Mr. Riggs."

(We play a few games and sing some songs. The family is obviously enjoying it.)

"Well, we've had a good time, haven't we kids? But before we go we'd like to tell you about a prophet."

(We tell him the Joseph Smith story and ask him how he feels about our message.)

"Well, it sounds logical, but like I said, you could never convert me. I haven't been in a church for years."

"We understand. We'd like to leave a copy of the Book of Mormon and have you read a few pages."

"You can leave it. Susan will read it, but I don't even read the Bible."

"You could read a few pages too, Honey," she says to him in a hopeful tone.

His attitude has changed. He likes us.

"Tell me more about those mule deer. Did you ever get one?"

We tell of a hunting venture or two and then I say, "We'll be back in the neighborhood Saturday night; we'll stop by then and see how you are doing."

"Sure. Come back anytime. You use rifles. That's really something."

SCENE III

It's Saturday night.

"Come in, Elders."

"Hi, kids. Can you remember how to do eensy weensy spider?"

"Look at this *Field and Stream*. Is this anywhere near your home? Look at those mountains."

"Did you read the pages?"

"No, I haven't had time. Susan read a little, didn't you?"

I ask with a smile on my face, "Mr. Riggs, how are you ever going to learn anything if you don't read?"

"As I said, you are welcome here but I'm just not much on religion. By the way, a fellow at work was really putting your church down. I told him he didn't know what he was talking about."

"We appreciate that. Tonight after we have a word of prayer we'd like to tell you some more about the Church."

"Sure, go ahead."

(Discuss more about the Book of Mormon.)

"What do you think of what we are telling you?"

"Well, it sounds good."

"Do you feel it's true?"

"I don't know. I guess it could be. What do you think, Susan?"

"I feel the same."

"Could we ask you again to read these pages of the Book of Mormon?"

"Yeah, I could read a little. Hey, my wife made some strawberry pie. Get some pie. Get us each a piece."

Mrs. Riggs starts to get the pie and as she does so she says: "Get down, Blacky. Elder Matthews doesn't want you on his lap while he eats pie."

"Oh, that's all right," I reply. "Elder Matthews really likes dogs."

"We shouldn't really stop to eat. But we'll make a sacrifice this time and stay a few minutes."

"We will see you on Monday night."

SCENE IV

(Monday night.)

"I was looking at rifles down to the sporting goods store. They have some nice ones but they cost a pretty penny."

"Did you read the pages?"

"Yeah, I did. It's sort of like the Bible, except I didn't know that Jesus came to people on this continent. It was a beautiful story."

"How did you feel about it?"

"I enjoyed it. I felt sort of religious while I was reading. Susan has read practically all of the book, haven't you, Honey?"

"No, not all. Maybe about half."

"Hey, is your church over on Eastern Parkway? I was riding by there yesterday and I saw some people going in there."

"That's our church, or at least one of them."

"Well, I was just wondering. I'm not going to come over there, but I thought that was the Mormons. That guy down at work keeps after you something fierce. I asked him if he'd ever read the Book of Mormon. He told me no, and he wasn't going to either. I asked him how he was ever going to learn anything if he didn't read."

(We then discuss eternal progression.)

"You know, Elders, I'm starting to feel religious. I didn't ever know all this stuff you've been telling us. The kids have been after me to go to church, but I just couldn't do that."

"Blacky, don't lick his hand."

"That's fine. Elder Matthews likes dogs."

"So that is your church. What time do you meet? I'm just curious."

"Before we go we'd like to pray again with you. Let's kneel down. Mr. Riggs, we'd like you to offer it."

"Me? I've never prayed out loud."

(We tell him what constitutes prayer and teach him how to pray.)

After he finishes, and as we arise from our knees, you say: "That was a great prayer, Mr. Riggs. Kids, if you want to know how to pray, ask your father. He knows how."

SCENE V

(Ten days later.)

"How did you like church?"

"The children really liked it. And I suppose I did too. Hey, I was surprised I know the bishop. He and I went to high school together. He works at General Electric. How does he do that and also be the bishop?"

"We were really thrilled to see you walk in. Your kids sure did look happy. We'd been praying that you'd come."

"You prayed that we'd come?"

"We sure did."

"Why?"

"I suppose it's because we have come to love all of you so much and because we know that the Church can make your family happier than you could ever be any other way. This is the Lord's church, Brother Riggs."

"I've been reading more in the Book of Mormon. Susan has read the whole thing."

"How do you feel about the Church and all we've told you?"

"You know, it's a funny thing, but I really feel good about it all. I feel that Joseph Smith really did see God and Jesus Christ. I told that guy down at work that. He just shook his head and walked off."

"Mr. Riggs, you know these things are true because the Holy Ghost is testifying to your soul that they are. Right now I can feel the Spirit and I'm sure you can, too."

"I can."

"I feel I should tell you that on the third of next month we are having a baptism. We'd like you and Sister Riggs to prepare to be baptized on that date. Will you be ready?"

"Well, I don't know. I haven't really been religious for so long. Susan, how do you feel?"

"I hope we can. It would be so good for the family. And we all know it's true. The children have said how much they like you Elders and how much they want to go to church again."

"What about it?"

"Well, I don't know. A month ago I wouldn't have even believed I'd feel this way. I suppose we could try."

"We'll count on it. We know the Lord will help you be ready."

"By the way, when this guy at work came back, I told him about the three degrees of glory. He hadn't even heard of that before."

Scene VI

A week later.

Elder Matthews is speaking: "Tonight we have a most important message. The Lord has given us some commandments which he expects us to live if we are to be members of his Church."

Mr. Riggs interrupts: "Before you go on could I ask a question? You Mormons, or I should say we Mormons, we don't smoke do we?"

"No, we don't."

"I knew it. I knew I'd have to quit. I just felt it. I've not smoked in three days."

"That's great. We also don't drink coffee."

"You don't? I mean, we don't? Well, anyway I suppose that's all right because I'm an iced tea man."

"We don't drink tea either!"

"You don't? What do you drink?"

"Water, milk, postum."

"Postum? What's that?"

"It's a grain drink."

"Is it any good?"

"Well, it's a . . . it's a . . . it's quite good."

"And of course we don't drink alcohol."

"You mean beer?"

"That's right."

"I'm a beer drinker from way back. I don't know if I can give that up."

"We're sure you can."

"I've got some cans in the fridge now."

"What you ought to do is get them out, and we'll pour them down the drain."

"Are you kidding?"

"Not really."

As the beer is being poured down the drain, Mr. Riggs says longingly: "What a waste! My friends would die if they saw all that beer going down the drain. That's the last one. You Elders really know how to change a guy's life, don't you?"

I add with a smile, "Well, it's more the Lord than it is us."

We continue on, "Tithing is 10 percent of one's income."

Mr. Riggs, in a dejected tone: "We could never do that. Money is a problem with us. What with our house payments, our car payments, and other things, we're going in the hole as it is."

Elder Matthews says, "Let's read from Malachi." (We do so.)

Elder Matthews speaks with some emotion: "Mr. Riggs, go ahead and test the Lord and see what happens. He'll bless you if you pay tithing. You can do it. We know that you can."

"It'll be hard. Susan, can we do it? Elders, when you speak, I just feel as if we can do anything."

SCENE VII

(The baptism.)

While standing in the water with Mr. Riggs I speak, "John Roy Riggs, having been commissioned of . . ."

After a glorious family baptism, we stand in a circle and talk. With tearful eyes Brother Riggs speaks: "Elders, thanks. What else can I say? Just thanks."

Members greet the new converts: "Welcome into the Church, Brother and Sister Riggs. Your oldest son was also baptized, and when your other kids are eight years old they will be baptized too."

Sister Riggs, in a voice louder than usual, says so that all can hear: "We love our missionaries. We want our children to grow up to be just like them."

SCENE VIII

A week later the Elders and the home teachers call on the Riggs family. "We've brought the home teachers again. They'll be visiting you now as they did the week before your baptism."

Almost in unison the Riggs family asks in concerned tones, "Where's Elder Matthews?"

I speak in a forced kind of cheerfulness, "He was transferred."

"Transferred? Why?"

"The president felt he was needed up north."

"But what about us? We can't get along without him." (Tears form in Brother Rigg's eyes.)

I speak up as I place my hand on my new companion's shoulder, "This is Elder Simmons."

"Blacky, get down."

"That's all right, Sister Riggs. Elder Simmons likes dogs."

SCENE IX

A little over a year later. A phone call to a college dormitory.
"What are you doing Friday?"
"I've got a test."
"Oh, too bad. I was hoping you could join Sister Riggs and myself and our five kids in the temple. We're being sealed."
"I'll skip the test."
Brother Riggs is overjoyed as he adds: "Good old Elder Matthews will be there too. He's going to bring his wife with him. It will be so good to be together again."

SCENE X

The group has just come out of the temple. Brother Riggs says with pride, "Hey, I didn't tell you, Elders, but I'm first counselor in the elders quorum."
Sister Riggs adds: "I'm so proud of him. You'd never believe the change. He treats me like a queen. He's really something."
Brother Riggs looks down and says humbly, "I'm not so much."
"Oh, yes you are, Sweetheart. You're the best man in the world."
I laughingly say, "You mean he's even better than old Elder Matthews and I?"
Sister Riggs smiles and says, "Just a little."
"Elders, Susan and the kids and I talk about you all the time. Without you we'd have missed everything."
"Johnnie here is going to be quite an Elder in eight years. We just hope he'll be like you two. We hope all our children will."
Brother Riggs looks toward the mountains. "Any deer up there do you think? You use rifles?"
I add, "Yeah, rifles."
I look at Brother Riggs. He looks back at me. We both start to laugh. It is either that or cry. It doesn't seem possible to be so happy.

5 / *Sisters*

I can see you in my mind. You are a missionary-age young woman. You are still a free agent with no immediate prospects for marriage and you have a big question, "Should I go?"

I can answer that question for you with ease and with just three short words, "I don't know."

But, of course, there is a better, more definite answer. It's an answer which is sometimes difficult to find, but it is there. To find it will require a lot of prayer, a good deal of counsel with parents, a heart-to-heart talk with priesthood leaders, and some long and thoughtful meditation.

And if the answer comes out yes, fasten your seat belt, grit your teeth and hang on. You are on your way to eighteen months of the hardest, most tiring, most frustrating, most discouraging, most taxing, most growing, most exhilarating, most meaningful of life's "thus-far" experiences.

To devote an entire chapter to Lady Missionaries could be considered unnecessary. After all, when it comes to missionary work, aren't you just like an Elder? Well, as a matter of fact, you are like an Elder and you aren't.

Let's ignore the ways that you are like an Elder and dwell on the ways that you aren't like your male counterpart.

In the first place, you are much prettier than an Elder. I've never seen a picture of a group of missionaries (and I've seen roughly seventeen billion such pictures) that was really a work of art unless there were at least two Lady Missionaries in the frame.

But being pretty isn't the entire story. Let's look beyond beauty and examine the behind-the-scene experiences you will have as a missionary.

Your mission may serve as a magnifying glass for your personal problems. Insecurities prior to a mission can seem larger while you are serving your mission. Lingering little health problems can become almost daily roadblocks to productive work. Weight problems can easily become weightier. Moodiness often becomes almost monstrousness. Lack of organization becomes almost chaos.

On the other hand . . . But that's positive. Right now we are being negative. We'll be more hopeful a bit later in the chapter.

Being with a companion twenty-four hours a day is sometimes quite stifling. Sometimes it seems more like a prison than does Fort Leavenworth. The day-after-day-after-day routine of rising early, tracting, teaching, studying, and memorizing can grind you down to nerve and bone.

But don't get discouraged. We have more to say than what we've said.

For example, let's look in on the mission president as he plans a transfer. Before he begins to plan this transfer he has prayed long and fervently. As we join him, he is looking at the big missionary picture board on his wall. On the board we see pictured 180 young Elders, 6 married couples, and 12 Sisters.

The president says to himself: "That does it for the Elders. Now what about the Sisters? Let's see, we have twelve Sisters. Sister West is going home next week. The week after that Sister Smedley and Sister Billings arrive. Who should I put with Sister Hensen when Sister West goes? And who would be good companions for Sisters Smedley and Billings? And where should I put their former companions?

"Let's see, I could put Sister Riggins with Sister Bester. But they were together before. Or I could put Sister Riggins with Sister Brith. But they are both quite new. Sister Dollins and Sister Smith are doing well together and if I divide them, I feel it will hurt Sister Dollins because she is doing better than ever before. So let's see. What about . . . ?"

We must leave the president now. He needs to be able to concentrate on the hardest of all transfers — the Sisters. The reason such moves are difficult is that the number of Sisters in the mission is not large. With the Elders there are hundreds of alternatives for companionship, but with the Sisters there are only a few.

Therefore, when Sister companionship is difficult, the president is rather limited in the possible transfers he can make. That demands that you and your companions sort out your difficulties together. Although that's the best way, it is also the reason Sister companionships are more difficult that Elder companionships. This is also the reason you are sometimes transferred back to a Sister with whom you have already labored. This may be thrilling to you unless you are going back to a companion whom you didn't really enjoy with all of your heart. On the other hand, you may be rejoining a Sister with whom you enjoyed a type of harmony that was almost heavenly.

But enough of this negative talk. There is so much good in store for you if you decide to cast your lot as a missionary. Just hearing the titles *Sisters* or *Lady Missionaries* brings into my mind a multitude of warm and joyful memories.

Let's go forward in our thinking and look in on you while you serve on your mission. There you are, a Lady Missionary, and by your side is your companion. You are smiling and you look more radiant than you've ever looked before. You ought to look tired because you've been working harder than you've ever done before. But somehow the work seems to produce a glow in your countenance. Your hair is neat and your makeup perfect. Your dress is modest and not in any way extreme. You may never have won a beauty contest, but right now you'd put Miss America to shame.

You are with a companion who is as energetic as you are. The two of you are among the mission leaders in work and in results. Some Elders are a bit jealous of you and could at times make disparaging remarks. Other Elders are determined to keep up with the Sisters and they begin to increase their labor. The mature Elders (and most of them are) come to deeply respect and admire you and the other Sisters.

You have found that doors closed to Elders are often open to Sisters. The feminine spirit makes for great teachers. And many Sisters are indeed known by the lofty description *master teacher*. In your own teaching you feel a power that you had never felt before your mission. Tears come to your eyes easily as you discuss sacred things. And so often lately the hearts of your listeners are touched.

You have come to sense more than ever before your own personal worth. Families in the ward to which you are assigned seem to respect you as if you were the source of all knowledge and virtue.

Your personal values have not changed, but you've learned to empathize because you've seen so many families with problems and so much heartbreak in the lives of others. Somehow such things have subdued your soul and caused you to be determined in your own pursuit of a righteous life.

Your appreciation for your parents increases. You can see now that even though they have had problems, they are striving. You love them so deeply that the thought of them warms your heart.

You are hurrying along because you have an appointment. And after that another appointment. When will the work let up so that you can rest? You wonder why you feel so eager when you should be so tired.

A smile crosses your face as you remember that in two more days you will be at zone conference. These glorious meetings are looked forward to more than college junior prom dances. It will be so good to see Sister Dollins and Sister Braithwait again. You hope the mission president's wife will be with him. She is one of your heroes.

So there you are, a Lady Missionary. What do you think? Do you want to try it?

Speaking of zone conferences — while serving as mission president I felt that a zone conference without at least one set of Sisters was like a Christmas without snow. You could still get the spirit but not the sparkle. The Elders weren't flirts but it's amazing how much more sentimental, mannerly, loving, and, above all, powerful they become when Sisters' eyes were looking on.

In my opinion the Sisters make a mission experience complete.

Of course, I'm biased toward Lady Missionaries because, you see, I married one. Statistically, the chances of your marrying an Elder you met in your mission are small. You need not have any fears in that regard.

The former Sister Burnham and I labored together in England. I arrived there three months before she did. I had picked up the language really fast and was an "old-timer" when she arrived. Come to think of it, I've never figured out how she could get there after I did, go home before I did, and still accomplish so much more than I did.

She has told me many times that the reason Lady Missionaries only stay out eighteen months is that they can do more in that time than an Elder can in two years. But I keep her humble by advising her that, even though she helped more people join the Church than I did, I baptized more people than she did. (I've got to defend myself some way!)

Selfishly speaking, I'm deeply grateful that she went on a mission. She learned so much there that has made my life with her blessed. For example, she learned how to get along with companions who weren't perfect (that has been a great help to me). She also learned how to live in a humble apartment, how to live on a very limited budget, how to walk and not complain, and how to run for a bus and not faint. She learned to pray with deep faith that a family she had come to love as her own would join the Church.

She learned about God and came to know him as her Heavenly Father. She came to know Jesus Christ and recognize that he indeed was her Savior. She learned to recognize the promptings of the Holy Ghost and the comfort of such an influence. She learned the power of faith, the hope and cleanliness of repentance, the urgency of baptism. She learned of charity and hope. She learned to pursue goals with all her heart and soul. She learned to speak and to teach. She learned to be calm in the midst of turmoil. In summary, she learned everything I had always hoped that my wife and the mother of my children would know.

So the decision is yours. It's a tough decision. It would be easy if someone else could decide for you.

I'll close the case by saying that I've never met a Sister who did go who would trade her experience for a fortune in gold. For this I know with a certainty; when the time is right, there is nothing more thrilling than being a missionary.

6 / The Couples

Of all aspects of a mission one might wonder what is the single most wonderful thing. I'm tempted to say (and I think I will say it) that the single most wonderful thing actually comes in sets — those marvelous couples who serve their missions together. They come to the mission two by two. They go forth that way and they return home together. For these reasons these most special missionaries are called the *couples*.

If you choose to become a missionary couple, you'll come with fear and trembling, wondering if you'll succeed. You'll return home among the greatest of all spiritual heroes and with success that goes beyond even your fondest dreams. At first you will be as strangers in an unfamiliar place, but when you depart for home you'll discover that your mission field is now your second home. You will wonder when you come what it will be like. Will success be yours? As you go home, you'll wonder humbly, "Can these people possibly carry on if we leave them?

How does it all begin? Often there is a lifelong desire. Put into words it goes like this. "Honey, someday when our circumstances are right, I'd love to serve a mission with you." Then when the children are raised, the time seems right. But there is another obstacle. What about the grandchildren? Could you ever leave them? You wouldn't even see them at Christmas. And then there is the house. What would you do with the house? And the garden. You have such a lovely garden. Besides, your health is far from perfect.

But then the bishop calls. "Could you both come in this evening and see me?" You question each other: "Will it be a call to serve in the ward? In the temple? Or will it be . . . ? No, it couldn't be that."

The bishop draws a deep breath. He has prayed about this, but now in this moment his courage almost fails him. He must ask so much of you. He makes small talk, and then: "My dear brother and sister, I have prayed much about this. I would like you to accept a call to serve a full-time mission."

A long silence follows. You look at each other. Your hands reach out and touch. Then in a quiet voice you ask, "When would we leave?"

"Perhaps a month, perhaps two."

"That would be just before Thanksgiving!"

"Honey, what do you think?"

"Well, it will be hard at our age, but I suppose that we've always dreamed that we'd go."

"But what of our health? The heart problem and all?"

"I'll be all right. The Lord will take care of us. And if something does happen, what better thing could we be doing?"

"You people are so dear to all of us here. We will miss you desperately. Your children and the grandchildren will miss you too. Do you want time to consider it?"

"No, no, Bishop! We'll go. We don't need time to think. We'll need a little time to get ready, but we don't need time to think. We've done that all our life."

A sleepless night. Fear and faith at war. Then the idea seems to feel more at home. A family gathering and an announcement.

"Kids, your mom and I are going on a mission."

There are embraces, tears, and the words: "That's so wonderful! You'll do great! The people will love you."

"Where will you go, Grandpa?"

"How long will you be gone?"

"Mamma, I don't want Grandma and Grandpa to go." Tears.

"Now, children. Heavenly Father needs them."

"But who will take me fishing and to the park?"

You have second thoughts, but only momentarily. "Grandpa and I will write to you. We'll send you pictures."

Time flies by. So much to get ready. So much to do.

The mailman with the call. "It's here, Honey. This is it. Sit down and let's open it. You open it. I can't quit trembling."

"Where does it say?"

"Let's see, it's to . . ."

"We've never even been close to there. Call the children and tell them."

Conversations with those who have lived there or who have relatives there. Pictures in encyclopedias.

All is ready. The house will be all right. Boxes are filled and stored.

At the farewell. "The chapel seems so full. I didn't know so many people would come."

After the meeting there are many kind words and tears.

Almost everyone tells you the same thing: "We'll miss you because we love you. You'll do great."

Back home after the meeting: "Wasn't that something, Honey. I never dreamed that many people would come. I didn't know they all loved us so much."

But these are the hardest good-byes ever said, (and saying good-bye is always difficult). When friends part, it's hard. When children leave parents, there are tears. But saying good-bye to the grand-children — that can't be described. Only something this important could give one the strength to endure such a tender parting.

Off to the missionary training center, more nervous than ever before. Other couples are there. You wonder how friendships could develop in a day that are as dear as those that have been nurtured for a lifetime. But these people, these other couples in the missionary train-ing center, become instant friends because of the common bond of emotion, fears, faith, and love.

The journey of many miles and finally you are almost there. What will the mission president be like? Will he ask more of you than you can give?

You meet him. He is so kind and understanding. You just met him and his wife and you love them already. You feel so much better now.

But where will he send you? Will the people there accept you? Where will you live? Will you even be able to find your way there? You don't know a living soul there. "I wonder if the house back home is okay. I hope the furnace works." A quick thought of your front room at home. The kitchen. The garden, the grandchildren. A surge of real homesickness fills your heart.

Finally there it is. There's your new city. The handsome young zone leaders meet you. These young men are so mature, so confident, so friendly.

"This is your apartment. If it's unsuitable, you can look around and get another."

So small. So humble, yet it seems so much like the right place.

Unpack.

The president of the small branch stops by. He seems so glad you are here.

The first week at church. Not a large group, but so humble, so full of appreciation. So many invitations to visit members. Such instant love.

"Please come by. My husband will want to meet you. I'll bet you are the ones who will get him into the Church."

Time goes by, but only slowly at first. Weeks, then months. The branch president asks for your advice on a number of matters. He wants to succeed but is so new in Church leadership. All the training we had in the Church at home means so much here where leadership is sparse. The president seems so appreciative of the support you give. The number of people at church increases. The spirit seems so much better now.

A baptism. Such a good husband and father. You've never seen a happier family.

Now you are teaching the man who works at the grocery store and also the postman. The landlord is also asking questions.

Your lives are entwining with other lives. Thoughts of home are less frequent.

A letter from home contains pictures of the children. They seem to have grown. You read: "Johnny said, 'My Grandma and Grandpa are on a mission. When I get big I'm going on a mission too.' "

You feel a joy which is unsurpassed.

Problems. These people need so much help. A long talk with a married couple headed for divorce. They seemed to feel better after the talk. "Oh, Heavenly Father, we love them so much. Please help them."

And then a crushing blow. It is a call from the mission president. A transfer. How can you leave here? Tears at a farewell party. You are ready to leave your apartment and your town. Many come to bid you good-bye. As you look into their tear-filled eyes, you say, "We'll be back — after our mission, we'll be back."

"God bless you," they call out to you. "We'll never forget you."

A new area. More confidence this time. The cycle starts again.

A call from home at Christmas.

"Grandpa, I can't wait until spring, 'cause Mom says you'll be home."

Spring is coming soon. Please slow down the time. You still have much to do. These people need a chapel. The president is trying so hard. The two factions of the branch seem to be coming together at last. You love it here. The family you taught and baptized is struggling, but they are determined to make it to the temple in a year.

This place is so beautiful. This little apartment is home. The flowers in the window are doing well.

The young Elders are like your own sons. You love to feed them. They rely on you a great deal. They are wonderful.

The president says he doesn't know what he'd do without you. He's such a good man.

The other ten couples and you met together for a conference. You decided you'd meet each year after your missions. You never have known such wonderful couples. They came here from Ohio, Michigan, California, Idaho, Arizona, Nevada, Indiana, Wyoming, and Utah. They were farmers, coal miners, lawyers, businessmen, hunting guides, handymen, and teachers. They all have grandchildren and gardens. You could talk with them forever. You love to get together with them, but at the end of such meetings you can hardly bear to say so long.

Sad news. One of the Elders whom you saw at the conference is in the hospital. He had a heart attack. But he told his wife he'd recover because he had received a blessing from the president. He's doing better. You are fasting and praying for him. He is a choice man and his wife is like an angel.

Time is closing in on you. A farewell party is planned. The grandchildren write often. They are so excited.

You'll be home in time to plant the garden — but somehow that doesn't seem as important as it once did. The people will move out of your house the week before you get home. What will you ever do with that big house? This little apartment seems just the right size.

The farewell party. A special song composed by a newly activated sister. The words are about you. They are words of love and appreciation. You both cry. You've never felt so needed, so loved.

Farewell talks. Power with words has never been like this. As you speak you express your feelings as best you can but then you pause, for no words will come. Then a testimony that has never been as strong.

The parting. It would be unbearable except for the hope in the words: "We'll come back. Don't worry, we'll come back." The journey away from the people you love. Going home is not what you thought it would be.

The homecoming. No one could really know how much the mission meant to you. From now on almost every conversation you will ever have will include a thought of the mission. Hoeing corn and washing dishes leave time for thinking. What did you ever think of or talk about before your mission?

"What if we'd never gone, Honey? What if we'd never met those folks?" The thought is too hard to bear.

Yes, you come two by two; you labor two by two; you perform miracles two by two. You fall more and more in love. You depend on each other. You know joy and sorrow two by two. You are loved by the people as one. And then when your mission is done, you head home to your first home. You now have a second home and almost a new family. Your life now will never be the same.

Yes, these are the couples. The special people who come and who care, who love and are loved, and who will be called blessed forever.

To them the word *mission* will always bring back many memories. May God bless the couples forever.

7 / *The President*

"Hello, Elder. I know it's early in the morning, but I was sure you'd be up."

"Oh, hello, President. I, ah, didn't recognize your voice there for a minute."

"Elder, we've got three missionaries going home next week and we need to do a little shifting. I've thought about it and prayed about it and I'd like to transfer you. Could you catch a bus tomorrow and go up to Nextsville?"

"I sure can, President. Who'll I be working with there?"

"You'll have a new missionary and I've not quite decided which one. You'll be senior companion and it's a new area. The Lord will bless you. Let me talk to your companion about who will be coming to work with him."

"Sure, President. And, hey, President, I just want you to know that I, ah, well, I — I love and appreciate you."

"Thanks, Elder. I share those same feelings for you."

A few moments later two excited missionaries prepare for the future, a future just set in motion by the most important man in their lives for two years — the mission president.

It's been some years since I served as a young missionary in England. But even now when I focus my mind upon my mission president, it sends a wonderful sensation through my soul. I can't remember all that he said in his public addresses but I can recall almost every word that he ever spoke to me personally and privately.

Just to have him greet me with his warm smile and a friendly "hello, Elder Durrant" could inspire me to want to be great. To know that he knew my name made me feel special. To hear him say "Elder Durrant, you are doing a fine job" would render me speechless because of my inward joy.

I was always nervous in his presence. That wasn't his fault but mine. I don't regret that I was uneasy in his company, because I'm not sure it was so much fear as it was respect. I simply stood in awe of this marvelous man whom I called *President*.

As a missionary, I loved the Lord with all my heart and I desired to please him. My mission president was the Lord's representative and when I reported to the president I felt as though I was reporting to the Lord.

As I write, I find that it is futile to try to put into words the feelings of joy that come into my heart as I remember my beloved president.

Many years later when I served as a president, my greatest motivation was my desire to have even one of my missionaries love and respect me as I had loved and respected my president.

But never during my three years as president did I dare to dream that anyone could actually ever feel about me as I had felt about my president.

I didn't try to be like my president because he and I are not the same in personality or experience, but I tried to be in my way what he was in his.

As I said in the introduction, you and I are alike in the feelings of our hearts. And, although I can't imagine your president being as great as mine was, I'm sure that your feelings for your leader will be much the same as mine were for mine.

I've always been a bit fearful of authority figures. Since my earliest recollection my insecurities made me wonder if I could measure up in the eyes of my teachers and leaders. My basketball coach made me so nervous that I couldn't even carry on a reasonable conversation with him (though I had many opportunities to do so because I spent each game sitting right next to him on the bench).

Just the knowledge that he could put me on or leave me off the list of newly chosen team members that hung on the wall in the gym caused me to almost tremble in his presence. And then all season long, knowing that at any moment he might say "George, get your sweat suit off and get in there" made me too nervous to look his way.

Later I felt much the same as I greased a car while my service station boss watched. He too made me nervous because I desperately needed to keep the job and deeply wanted to please him.

With my mission president it was the same, only it was different. The many ideals which are so much a part of a mission experience made words such as *trust, respect, confidence* more important than things I had formerly dreamed of and which bore labels such as *popular* and *all-state*. Whereas before I had dreamed of personal glory and applause, now my most intense desire was that my president would think well of me.

You, because you are a little different from me, may not fear authority figures. You might say: "Why be nervous around anyone, including the president? After all, he's a person just like me." The honors you have achieved and other fulfilling events in your past experience might have so filled your life that you stand in awe of no man. But as your mission unfolds even you will, if you are truly blessed, come to have a great respect for your president. And you too will feel a special tingle of excitement as you enter a private room to be interviewed by this man who has so much to do with all your mission hopes and dreams.

Mission presidents are as different from one another as are missionaries. Some are what I would call "tough," others are "soft." Some could be called conservative in desiring each missionary to "toe the line." And others are more lenient in the specific direction given to their Elders and Sisters. Some are more adept at teaching and others have talents in organizing and administering programs that make things move. Some are constantly praising the missionaries. Others give few compliments. Some have been businessmen, some teachers, some doctors, some lawyers, and some farmers.

One of the most exciting and important things about your mission will be which of all of these kinds of men you will get as a mission president. And it's my belief that you'll get just exactly the right one for you.

I recall that shortly after I had received my call to serve as president, an old high school friend came by to see me. He had seen my picture in the *Church News*. We visited for a while and as he departed he said: "George, you'll have a hard time for the next three years. You're too soft to be president. Those missionaries will run all over you."

His words worried me. I fully realized that I was not a talented boss. Giving and enforcing orders was not something I felt comfortable doing.

As young missionaries approach their missions, they worry and wonder. So do mission presidents. I've never approached a task with more apprehension. I, of course, prayed often, and as I did I'd think of my mission president.

I would recall that he never forced me to do anything. But, oh, how he loved me, trusted me, respected me, and made me want with all my heart to help him fulfill his desires. As a result, I loved him as I'd never loved anyone before. And now, as I considered my mission, I wanted to govern others as he had governed me.

I once had the thrill of seeing the movie *Camelot*. The story of King Arthur and the knights of the Round Table is fiction, but the principles which it teaches ring with truth. The movie portrayed a glorious kingdom known as Camelot. For a few short years King Arthur reached heights of government never known before or since. He had the perfect order. All motivation was pure. Unity abounded.

As my mission came nearer, I was determined that with God's help I would be the King Arthur of a spiritual Camelot. I looked upon my mission as an opportunity for a grand and wonderful experiment in trust, respect, and love. I determined that I would strive to govern by establishing and teaching true principles. I would allow each missionary considerable freedom in deciding for himself his conduct as it related to these principles. Punishment for wrong choices would only come after the realization that a trust had been broken and respect had been damaged. Rewards for right choices would bring personal satisfaction and the knowledge that the respect of self and leaders would be enhanced.

I knew that Sir Lancelot betrayed King Arthur and thus destroyed Camelot. I decided that I'd risk my Lancelots. If someone took advantage, then that would have to be. Such betrayals might bring isolated cases of heartache but would not be a sufficient reason to abandon the grand and exciting experiment of establishing another "Camelot."

The instruction and inspiration I received at the mission home in Salt Lake City softened my heart and prepared me for a spiritual experience which came near the closing of the mission president's conference. We all stood and began to recite together the fourth section of the Doctrine and Covenants. After speaking a line or two, my soul was completely filled. I could say no more. The Lord spoke to me, assuring me that by using the principles I harbored in my heart, I could succeed as a mission president.

And so it is with all presidents. Each is called because of what he is. And if he couples his strengths with the Spirit of the Lord, he will not fail.

As I arrived in the mission field, I wondered, "Will the missionaries accept me?" I quickly found that they would. I began to learn that missionaries have an intense desire to want to love their president. If he is just an average sort of person, they make him great in their minds.

I'll always remember my arrival in Nashville. Nearly forty Elders were waiting. They were all lined up to meet me. As I passed down the line, each gripped my hand tightly and told me his name. We looked into each other's eyes and souls. In meeting them and discerning that they needed me, I was transformed from a man to a mission president. For the next three years I was different than I'd ever been before. Later in private interviews many hearts were opened to me. Tears were shed. I was overwhelmed at the trust my missionaries and the Lord had placed in me. The Spirit filled my bosom as I gave them counsel. These missionaries, these handsome noble spirits in the full armor of God, would do well for the knights of my "round table." Being treated and accepted even better than a king, I knew that my spiritual Camelot had officially begun.

I know of no other president who ever desired to be a second King Arthur, but each president I have known has had his own type of dream. And each reaches toward that dream in his own way.

Speaking, teaching, interviewing, transferring, praising, traveling, reorganizing, loving, inspiring, laughing, crying — all these are part of a president's life as he strives to achieve his dream. And of course each president hopes with all his heart to be inspired. For without the help of the Lord, spiritual dreams can't come true.

It always brought me deep introspection when I'd hear missionaries say, "I know that our president is inspired." Once we were all in a session of zone conference wherein I had invited each missionary to say just what he or she thought. Two Elders were a little disgruntled because of a recent transfer and each said that he didn't know if the president was inspired. Another Elder stood up. I recall he cried at first. Then he was able to speak. He physically trembled as he bore a testimony that brought a spirit into the room which I'll never forget. He said, "I know that the president is inspired." That was the greatest testimony ever borne in my behalf. He spoke with all the strength of his convictions. I was never able to look at that Elder again without thinking about that testimony and the strength it had given me. I felt that what he said was true, for I knew that the Lord was inspiring me each day.

Of transfers I wrote this in my journal:

"It's a great responsibility to transfer the missionaries. I desire with all my heart to put each one where he or she can best serve. I've made several new leaders and have given some their first opportunity to be senior companions. It would be easy if they were all unknown pawns, but each is a delicate personality who desires and deserves special care and consideration. It's a miracle we succeed as well as we do. I pray we will do the right thing."

While making transfers I've heard the voice of the Lord in my mind on many occasions. All the rest of the time I've had complete confidence that the Lord would not let us go astray. Once while I was conducting a meeting I was suddenly impressed to call one of the Elders out of the audience to come up to where I was speaking. I put my arm around him and told him he was the new assistant to the president. He was a little shocked by all this and, quite frankly, so was I. I guess the Lord was the only one who wasn't.

All who sincerely and intensely seek a lofty dream will find many dark days along the way, and so it is with mission presidents. From my daily journal I quote:

"I woke up discouraged. I felt tired physically but I believe it's mostly emotional. This is quite a task, and when I think about the responsibility I sometimes let it eat on me a little. I prayed and felt better. I helped the Elders mow and rake the lawn — it was good to do that kind of work. I played with the kids. Marilyn cut my hair. She does much better than a barber. She's a remarkable person. Tonight I prayed a long prayer. I'm concerned about mother's health. I felt better after the prayer. I feel more hope tonight."

Whenever things seemed a little bleak, the Lord always had something happen to help. One night I wrote:

"I was already a bit depressed last night when the phone rang. I wondered, 'What now?' It was two Elders who had called me the day before because they were having trouble getting along with each other. They said: 'We just felt we should call. We've settled our differences and we love each other. We wanted to tell you that we love you and we're sure glad that you are here.' When they hung up, I realized how much I had needed that phone call. Joy filled my heart as I rested my head on my pillow, smiled, and went to sleep."

All presidents desire to see many people join the Church, but even more intently they desire to be close and helpful to their beloved missionaries. Among the tasks of the president is the opportunity to interview his missionaries.

In a letter to the missionaries I once expressed myself on the subject of interviews:

"Dear Missionaries:

"Many times my thoughts and my prayers have centered on you — just you. I've always needed to know that those who presided over me cared for me and recognized that I had worth. No one could treat me more cruelly than to let me know that I didn't matter to him. I've tried to relate to you just as I like others to relate to me. But with all my desires and prayers, I know that sometimes it has been difficult for some to relate to me or to talk to me. For that I'm sorry.

"I've always felt that the time to give directive counsel was when I addressed all of you in a group. Such talks have often been centered on what I thought were your feelings, needs, weaknesses, and strengths. Then in the interview with you, I've tried to listen and perceive how you felt about what I'd said and about your personal status, goals, and desires.

"I recall that most of my interviews were not so much on the work as they were on you. I wanted to hear about your memories and your future dreams, about your parents and everything that you hold dear. When I could communicate on that basis, I felt that I came to know you. Often I could tell that as you left our private meeting that you had been inspired, and very often when you left I too had been inspired."

Reading again that letter brought to my mind some other memories associated with my private talks with individual missionaries. I recall that sometimes as I interviewed a discouraged or unmotivated missionary, I wouldn't know how to help him, and I'd almost give up. Then in my mind I'd envision my own son sitting where the Elder was sitting. I always used my son Warren for this purpose. When I saw the Elder as my son Warren, somehow things changed and I refused to give up; and then I was able to help.

I always tried to be worthy to listen to a missionary's words which reflected a broken heart and a contrite spirit. I've known the great responsibility that comes in being the only one who could open certain necessary doors for him or her which could lead to freedom from sin.

I believe that as mission president my first and foremost duty was to sit with a missionary in a private place and talk. All else seemed secondary to that. Office work and other duties were always essential and pressing, but only at zone conferences each five or six weeks did I feel that I was truly about my Father's business.

Interviewing, teaching, planning, and a multitude of other duties when coupled with family duties keep a mission president quite busy. And under such circumstances time flies by. Soon I had been out a year, then two, and then my time came near its close.

I recall now some of my thoughts as I neared the end of this most glorious experience of being mission president.

My thoughts as my days became numbered are best expressed in a talk which I gave on the occasion of my last meeting with the missionaries. To them I said:

"I've loved you, my missionaries. My love hasn't always been a perfect love and it has never been as intense for you as it has been for my own children. But nonetheless I've loved you deeply.

"A few years ago when my son Dwight (we call him Crow) was younger I took him from Salt Lake to Provo. While I worked at BYU he played with friends in the neighborhood where we had once lived. At day's end I picked him up and we drove toward home. We stopped for a snack. We took our order from the cafe and walked about twenty-five yards to the bank of the Provo River. There, sitting on a log we ate. I looked at the river and then at Crow, who was on the other end of the log.

"I spoke. 'I've got a better hamburger than you.'

"He answered, 'Mine's just like yours.'

"I added, 'My milkshake is better than yours.'

"He replied, 'Mine's the same flavor as yours.'

"After a pause I looked at him and said, 'I've got one thing that you haven't got.'

"He was certain that I didn't have, and asked with a challenge, 'What?'

" 'I've got a son that I call Crow. And I'm sitting on a log with him and I love him with all my heart. And you don't have that.'

"Crow didn't answer. He just looked at me for a few seconds, then he bit into his hamburger and threw a rock in the river. I had him, and he knew it.

"I've also got something you missionaries haven't got. I've got nearly two hundred missionaries whom I love and admire in a manner that I had never before dreamed possible. And with all the blessings you have, you don't have that. Now take another bite of your peanut butter sandwich, throw a rock in the river, and go forth.

"And now, as the final few pages are turned on this grand experience, my vision of Camelot is almost fulfilled. To say I have no regrets would be to speak an untruth. I've erred at times. But such mistakes resulted from lack of judgment and never from lack of desire to do right.

"I'm not a talented boss. But now I know that although bossing can work, there is indeed another way. I've also learned that a missionary, although partly a boy, is mostly a man. And as a man he will respond positively to love, respect, and trust. He will respond in righteousness not because he has to, but because he wants to.

"I make no claims to being the best of mission presidents when compared to others. My fame is personal and lives mainly in my heart. My vision of an almost perfect order was never one in which I felt I could avoid all problems but was instead a vision of an almost perfect way of dealing with problems. I knew things wouldn't be easy. I simply felt that by teaching correct principles, I could allow missionaries freedom to govern themselves. I knew that some, at some time, would take advantage, and such has indeed been the case. But all in all, I have much cause to rejoice and little cause to regret.

"Perhaps even King Arthur's Round Table was not all that he thought it was, but the important thing is that to him it was. And now in my heart I feel I've achieved my spiritual Camelot, and that makes me very, very happy.

"In the movie, King Arthur saw his Camelot ending by its internal destruction. In his parting from the place he loved, he told a young boy:

'Don't let it be forgot, that once there was a spot
For one brief shining moment that was known as Camelot.'

"For me, I'll think about and talk about that brief shining moment of my life when I experienced my spiritual Camelot.

"So now my kingdom here is ending. Its end comes not because of troubled circumstances, but because of time. My time has run out. Soon there will be a new King Arthur and perhaps a more perfect order. I long for the success of the future. But the future here will be without me. And that thought causes me sorrow.

"For me, there are other dreams. But perhaps never again will I stand upon such holy ground with such noble souls as you at my side. This experience has made its mark on my heart. Time will magnify the joy of my memories rather than erase them. The words *Kentucky* and *Tennessee* will pass my lips often as time goes by. And as they do my emotions will rise, a smile will cross my face, and in my mind I will be with you again.

"Tennyson, while recounting the fall of Camelot and the fatal wounding of King Arthur, had one of the last great knights, Sir Bedivere, ask:

> 'Ah! my Lord Arthur, whither shall I go?
> Where shall I hide my forehead and my eyes?
> For now I see the true old times are dead,
> When every morning brought a noble chance,
> And every chance brought out a noble knight.
> Such times have been not since the light that led
> The holy Elders with the gift of myrrh.
> But now the whole Round Table is dissolved
> Which was an image of the mighty world;
> And I, the last, go forth companionless,
> And the days darken round me, and the years,
> Among new men, strange faces, other minds.'
> And slowly answer'd Arthur from the barge:
> 'The old order changeth, yielding place to new,
> And God fulfills himself in many ways,
> Lest one good custom should corrupt the world.'

"Yes, indeed, the 'old order changeth, yielding place to new, and God fulfills himself in many ways.'

"And so farewell my mighty men and women — my dear friends. Because you helped me fulfill my dream, I shall never forget you. May God's choicest blessings be yours forever. All I ask now is your total support for the new order and just a little corner of your mind wherein you can store a slight memory of me."

8 / *Coming Home*

The English have an old saying which states, "Go to sea, son, if for no other reason than the glory of coming home."

Multiply a seaman's homecoming by a thousandfold and you'll catch at least a dim vision of the glory of a returning missionary.

When my son returned home from his mission, we were all at the airport an hour in advance of the scheduled arrival of his plane. As I waited, I found myself unable to carry on a sensible conversation. I had never been so nervous. I call it nervousness, but I'm not sure that is what it was. It was an undescribable inner emotional sensation that only comes a few times in an entire lifetime. And the closer the time of his arrival came, the more the wonderful sensation intensified within my soul.

I found myself wondering: "What will I do? What will I say? How will I act?"

On schedule the plane touched down. Through the glass windows I watched the doorway of the huge jet come open. People began to pour out. My son was not the first to disembark, nor was he among the first ten. I panicked a little as I wondered, "Did he miss the plane?"

I pressed my nose against the glass pane and counted — out came twenty more passengers. He was still not among them. I almost shouted at my wife: "Are we in the correct place? Is this the right flight?"

Fifty more exited — then a hundred more and a thousand (at least it seemed that many). Then came a break in the flow of deplaners and no more came. All of us who awaited were speechless. My so-called excitement had now become concern.

A second or two later the pilot came out. Then the ramp was empty again. But wait, another surge of hope. Two more passengers appeared and came down the stairs.

And then after another second or two, when I was sure he would not come, he appeared. With bags in hand and looking down to be sure of his step, he walked down the stairs to the ground and then he began to walk the thirty or so yards to the terminal. I watched his every step. I was spellbound at seeing him.

He came through the door. His seven brothers and sisters surrounded him. A broad smile crossed his face. His mother greeted him warmly.

And from my rearward position I came ever closer. Somehow the other family members stood aside and soon I stood face to face with my son. I looked into his eyes. And without any outward reasoning I embraced him and held him close to me, and I cried.

I had wondered what I'd do and now I knew. The only way to properly express all of my feelings was to throw aside all words and just hold him close and cry with joy. We had walked nearly to the baggage claim before I could speak any coherent sentences.

I've never been involved in anything so thrilling as the return of my missionary son.

And so, as a spokesman for all fathers and all mothers, I say to you, "Go on a mission, son, for a million reasons, among which is the glory of coming home."

Some chapters back I told of a newly arrived missionary who asked, "When does our mission begin?" On that occasion the mission secretary held his hand up above his head and looked at his watch. When the second hand swept to twelve, he dropped his hand and said, "Your mission begins now – Go!"

The newly arrived missionary is often convinced that two years will last forever. He reasons to himself, "The world will come to an end before my mission does." Inwardly he sometimes thinks: "Oh, if I could just rip the pages off the calendar and go home now. What a hero I would be! All would shout, 'There he is.' " Just the thought of going home is almost more than his heart can endure.

But two years do go by, and the 730-day absence is not as long as it looked at the beginning.

Missions are at first measured in hours, then days, and finally weeks. At first memories are all of home. But gradually there are memories of "when I landed," "the first discussion I ever taught," "the Applegate family," "my first area," "my first Christmas," and finally, "my first year."

That which seemed as if it would never end is at first a week old, then a month, then six; and finally, "I can't believe it — I've been here a year!"

As time goes by, it seems to gain momentum and becomes a speedster. And the missionary begins to realize that all really vital memories are now in the mission field. Getting together with old companions and contacts is like going home.

Time almost becomes a secondary issue. There is so much to do. Mission life is second nature now. You still have struggles in getting up in the morning, always being spiritually in tune, keeping your mind pure. But your motives have changed and your desire to conquer all personal weaknesses and flaws is intense.

As your mission passes by, you discover that somewhere, somehow, you have changed. This letter to my missionaries attempts to describe what happens:

"Dear Missionaries,

"Spring comes so gently. You have to watch the bushes and trees each day or else spring will be all about you and you'll never know just when it came. Personal growth is like that. You can't really tell that today you are different than yesterday, but you are or at least you can and ought to be.

"When your time here is over, you'll be as different as the trees of May are from those of February. Your limbs and roots will be the same, but you'll be covered with the leaves of spiritual growth.

"People at home will say of you: 'He hasn't changed and yet he has . . . he's still fun and funny, but he's . . . well . . . he's different. We see him now as one who teaches us instead of us, him. We see him counseling instead of being counseled. We see him as one to whom we can turn. Someone upon whom we can rely. Why, he'd sure make a fine bishop. As a matter of fact, someday I'll bet he'll . . .'

"Our mission is the spring of life. Experiences of sunshine and rain really do gently change us. We are warmed with a love for others that we've never known before. We are dampened by discouragement and by the day-by-day demand to stick to it. We sit on mountain peaks and descend into deep crevasses. Through it all we grow.

"Spring is here. Things are changing. The trees offer no resistance to the Creator and so they grow. The key to their growth, and to ours, is harmony with the Father.

"Put your hand into his hand. Gently say, 'Let thy will be my will.' And then go forth into the sun and grow."

Your time is now flying by. You've been out eighteen months and suddenly it's twenty months. "Slow down time, please." Then twenty-two months.

You are now one of the "old men" of the mission. A new missionary says to you, "How long have you been out?"

You reluctantly say, "Over a year."

He asks how much over a year.

Because of your honesty, you finally feel compelled to say, "I've been here twenty-two months."

He gasps for breath and says in complete awe, "Twenty-two months!"

He almost reaches out to touch you. You're a patriarch. You're the person to whom others turn for advice, for counsel, for encouragement. You, who have met and discussed the gospel with ministers, doctors, and governors. Your president has placed trust in you, and you've been true to that trust. Your scriptures are well marked and worn. You humbly know that you are respected and loved.

Finally there are only twenty days left. Then ten. Then only hours.

You meet with the president for the last time. Just the two of you alone. He says: "It seems as if it were just last week that I met you at the plane, and now you are going home. How do you feel knowing that tomorrow you'll be home?"

Your reply: "President, I'm confused. When I first came, I thought it would never end. And now I just can't believe it's over."

A long pause follows as you look into the president's eyes and he, into yours. A communication goes between you that can take place only between those whose love and respect is complete.

"You've been a valiant one, Elder."

"I've tried, President. I really have. I've not always been perfect and I've wasted a little time now and then, but I've tried. When I first came out, I wanted desperately for the time to fly by so that I could go home. I missed my folks and everyone at home. Out here I've found myself. I've discovered who I am and what life is all about."

"President, I didn't know I could ever love any place the way I love this place. I didn't know that I could get so close to people. These people are my people. I don't want to leave them. I feel like they need me. I wish I could stay, but at the same time I want to go home. I know there are things for me to do at home, but my heart is here."

Tears fill your eyes as you try to continue. "President, I'm confused. I want to go and I want to stay. What do you think?"

"Elder, your work here is finished. In the past two years you've captured some spiritual ground. Go home and never give up an inch of it. Let the bishop know you are ready to serve. Let basketball, cars and all else take a second seat. Let me read you a letter from Elder Smith.

" 'I've been home a month now. My dad put me to work first thing milking cows and farming. Just so you'll know I haven't gone inactive in the Church, I'm going to give you a run down on what I've been doing the last month. I've spoken in three ward sacrament meetings, twice to the seminary classes, twice at firesides, taught seventeen discussions, have one convert, and fed the church cows one week. This Sunday in priesthood class I'm going to start teaching the seventies how to use the missionary lessons. I'm not bragging. Just thought you would be happy to know that the Kentucky-Louisville Mission and all the people that go with it have saved another soul — mine.

" 'Love,

" 'Elder Smith' "

The president continues: "Yes, it's time to go home, my dear friend. I'll miss you here. We all will, but your life is now to go down different roads. Along the way you'll meet the right one and marry her in the right place. You'll become a counselor in the elders quorum presidency. You'll become a father. You'll move to the Midwest or someplace. You'll become a counselor in the bishopric. Another child will come. You'll fall more and more in love with your sweetheart. You'll be a great father.

"In other words, you have a destiny out there. Now square your shoulders. Go home and get on with life."

The two of you arise from your seats. You embrace this man who has come to mean so much.

"President, I thank you with all my heart. My mission has been . . . well it's just been everything."

And later, when the plane takes off, you look down on the holy ground where you found your "burning bush" and your "sacred grove." The miles flow beneath you and then the plane lands.

A father cries. You are home. There is much glory but it's not like you thought it would be nearly two years earlier. There's too much of you left behind in the "best" mission in the world. And because of what you left behind, you have brought much with you. You are now a man.

To hear the word *England* brings to me a million memories — street meetings, the milkman, bicycles, rows of houses, rain, testimony, President Reiser, Bilton Grange, President Audry, the Adams family.

And after serving as mission president I cannot hear the words, "Oh, the sun shines bright on my old Kentucky home," without wanting with all my heart to be there in Kentucky.

The word *mission* along with *love, father, mother, family,* tops the list of my dearest words. May God bless you that this mighty word may through personal experience send deep roots into your heart too.

In England we said, "Cheerio."

In the South it was, "Ya'll."

Thanks for being my companion and sharing your time and your feelings with me. I love you as only missionary companions can love. Until we meet again, without showing partiality to either of my missions I bid you farewell by saying, "Cheerio, ya'll."

APPENDIX

Newsletters to the Missionaries

At least once each month, and sometimes more often, I would write a message to all of the missionaries. We called such messages *Newsletters*. Thirteen of these messages are here included.

DIGNITY AND RESPECT

Some concepts are hard to express and are difficult for some to understand. So it is with the concepts which we describe with the word *dignity* and its twin *respect*.

A missionary showing dignity and respect calls his companion "Elder Clark." He knows that that is more appropriate than calling him "Clark" or "Robert" or "Robbie." He just senses that. No one needs to remind him. He calls his president, "President" rather than "pres." He does that because his inward dignity and respect causes him to sense that that is the way it should be.

His manners are most gracious. Words such as *thank you, excuse me*, and *please* come quickly and sincerely. In someone's home he sits with dignity. He's not a slouch; nor does he loosen his tie or try to act as though he's right at home. Because he knows he isn't.

He trifles not with sacred things. He smiles and he laughs, but always with dignity and respect. He handles his scriptures, his garments, his body with dignity and respect.

He doesn't want the self-criticism that comes from a poor performance, and thus he prepares and works so that his dignity and self-respect are totally intact.

Preserve your dignity and self-respect. No one else can do it for you. I humbly pray that you understand these vital concepts.

PRESSURE

Our first-string center had just fouled out. The coach had no one to turn to but me. Not much time remained when I left the bench upon which I had spent almost all of my basketball career. With only seconds remaining the score was tied and I was fouled. All eyes were upon me as I placed my toe as close as I could to the line. Pressure bore heavily upon my shoulders. Dear old American Fork High could win or lose, depending upon me. I released the ball and . . .

Well, you don't have to hear any more of that. But pressures are always upon those who go to the line and attempt to do great things. Every act of faith carries with it built-in pressure. Often faith requires an inward commitment that you are going to do something that is beyond your normal ability. And after a decision of faith you must ask yourself the soul-searching, pressure-packed question, "Can I do it?"

This kind of pressure is now associated with a decision you made that you will accomplish certain very difficult goals associated with helping people accept the gospel and become members of the Church. After the decision comes the pressure. Pressure to be clean in mind and body. Pressure to study and learn. Pressure to pray with fervor and meaning. Pressure to be more than you've ever been before. Pressure to be worthy so that the Lord can do his work through you.

If you set no such goals, you feel no pressure. There are those who say: "Oh well, I'm not going to worry. If we find someone, we will teach him; and if we don't, we won't." Or: "I do my best, and if they drop us they drop us. I'm not going to sweat it." To such people there is no pressure because there are no goals and thus no act of faith.

Pressure need not wear us down. It need not keep us awake at night. It need not cause us to have a nervous stomach. Pressure shouldn't break us down, it should build us up. Pressure is the soil in which great deeds grow. The way to handle pressure is found in the words of the song "Cast Your Burdens on the Lord." There's a difference in casting your burdens on the Lord and not having any burdens. We should have goals and commitments to achieve certain things. Things beyond our ability. Things that put us under pressure — calm motivating pressure — and which prompt us to work and to pray with all our heart.

Missions make us better because missions are filled with pressure. And when we respond positively to that pressure, we grow.

I'm grateful for pressure. Oh, that foul shot. Well, what do you think?

JOY IN THE GOSPEL

The assistants and I were driving north toward Nashville after having spent two days in Chattanooga. A carload of young men came up behind us rather rapidly and pulled alongside us. They looked over at us. We were dressed in our white shirts and ties. They were dressed differently. We thought at first that they were determined to cause us some trouble. But then they held up a book for us to see. We read the title *Mormon Doctrine*. Excitement filled both cars as we realized the great kinship that exists among Mormons.

Oh, it's great to be a Mormon! I don't believe any club or any group or any religion binds people together like our glorious Church. Go into a community as a stranger, meet another Mormon, and it's almost as if you're home again.

To be baptized and cleansed from sin; to dream of a temple marriage; to anoint with oil; to eat with a Mormon family; to read the Book of Mormon; to obey the Word of Wisdom; to hear the Brethren speak at conference; to be at a family home evening; to pay tithing; to fast and pray; to believe we lived as spirits before earth life; to know we can go back with our families to our Father in heaven; to have every thought tempered to some degree by the great revealed truths — all these things and a million more make me want to cry unto all: *"I'm a Mormon. I'm so glad that I am. Come and join us. It's a fountain of living water. It quenches all thirsts."*

We're called Mormons. But if people could see into our hearts, they'd see written there the name *Jesus Christ*. I guess that's why it's so good to meet another Mormon.

INSPIRATION

The other morning I read a thought that touched me deeply. Mormon, recounting past history, said of Helaman's sons Nephi and Lehi that they had "many revelations daily." (Helaman 11:23.)

I bear you my testimony that I too receive many revelations daily. Let me tell you of those I received yesterday.

I arose at 5:00 A.M. to prepare to go to the Lexington Stake Conference. I knew I'd speak there. I wanted to know what the Lord would have me say. I knelt in prayer. The Lord didn't tell me what to say, but as I concluded the speaking part of the prayer and paused to listen, he did speak to me in my heart. An inner voice said to me, "George, I love you." Joy filled my heart. This was a revelation that filled my soul with courage.

At Lexington I spoke to the priesthood leaders. As I spoke, the idea came to me that, just as the righteous Nephites were preserved through the destruction, so will the righteous of our day be preserved through any crisis that might come. This filled my soul with comfort. I felt my words take on power. I knew the Lord had spoken to me and I had repeated his words to my beloved friends.

In the general session I spoke again. Only two minutes were mine. I've never been so moved at the pulpit. I spoke of the love of Christ that brought about the Atonement. The Lord caused tears to come to my eyes as I told the people that I knew that we could make it all the way — all the way back to our Father's presence — if we would be obedient. I know that the Lord had told me what to say and had filled my soul with love.

We gave Elder Bennett, the visiting authority, a ride back to Louisville where he was to catch his plane. We talked of many things as we rode along. He thrilled Sister Durrant, Kathryn (our daughter) and myself and filled our souls with faith.

Then at the airport I told him good-bye. As we shook hands and he looked into my eyes and I into his, a spirit welled up within me. A spirit of love and joy. The Lord whispered to me, "He is indeed one of my choice servants." I knew that I was with a man of God.

We went home and later that day we attended sacrament meeting. Matt (our seventeen-year-old son) drove us there. He caught another ride home and took the keys to our car with him. As we sat later in the car that would not start without a key, I found myself wishing that Matt would receive a few more revelations daily. But then after all else that had happened that day, I smiled. Somehow a car that wouldn't start didn't seem very important.

Beloved missionaries, I humbly pray that you and I will receive many revelations each day.

WORK

Doing one's best isn't an impossible dream. We aren't talking of perfection. We have obstacles that block us short of that. Our best comes in fighting our way through colds, flat tires, and companion differences, and in coping with girls we want to love us who don't and girls we don't want to love us who do. We can't expect the wind to always be with us or all hills to slant downward. We must be able to move forward against the current. Thus, our best is not measured in results so much as in effort.

Bursts of speed are refreshing, but the work here is long and it demands a steady and methodical effort. The law of averages guarantees the success of the persistent.

I love you. I try to write my feelings, but words always seem to miss the real target. All I really want to say is "Do good and be happy." We just have to do the work. There's no one else to do it, and we are the Lord's agents. Our hands and hearts hold the keys to everything.

SPEAKING UP

I saw a young man at McDonalds. He was eating a hamburger, and I, a Big Mac. His hair was short and he wore a white shirt and tie. I came within a gnat's eyelash of saying: "Hi, there. I was wondering if you are a Mormon missionary?"

He would have said, "No, I'm not."

Then I'd have said, "Well, you sure look like an Elder in the Mormon Church."

"Do I?"

"You sure do. You look like a real winner, and that's the way they look."

"Well, thanks for the compliment."

"Anyway, I'm a Mormon missionary. What do you know about the Mormons?"

"Not much."

"Seeing as how you look like a missionary, I'm going to have two of them come by your home and see you. What's your address?"

And then the Elders would have taught him, and then he'd have been baptized and his wife and her parents and her uncle. And this man's sons would have gone on missions and . . . But all of this won't happen because I only *thought* of saying something. Then I thought I'd better eat my Big Mac and keep my thoughts to myself.

Now, as I think back, I feel terrible. I wish I could be back there at McDonalds and have a second chance. But I can't go back. I feel sad that I missed it. I humbly pray that I'll never miss such an opportunity again.

What about you? You deserve to give someone a break today at

McDonalds. Don't miss your opportunity to build a golden arch from someone to the truth.

ATTITUDE

I believe we all have the right to feel bad. I feel we will often have that privilege while we serve as missionaries.

When someone rejects us at his door, we should feel bad. When someone turns us away after a discussion or after they have lifted our hopes, we should feel deeply hurt. When someone almost decides to be baptized and then turns away, we should cry within our soul.

Some build defenses against such hurts. They say: "Oh, well, they had their chance." "We did our best." "Don't worry, this is just a hard mission." "It isn't our fault." "I didn't come out here to get all worried." "Noah didn't do so well either."

Sometimes we joke ourselves into an almost I-don't-care attitude. When that happens, we lose the edge that makes us ever desirous for the better way. If it's been a long time since you helped someone to baptism and that doesn't hurt you, you need to examine your goals.

There is a balance that makes life bearable and yet progressive. True, when we try hard and see little success, we shouldn't get down on ourselves; but if such results don't make us feel bad, we need to reevaluate that which we call our heart.

Among my greatest sorrows are the disappointments I knew as a missionary in England. Once after losing several contacts in one neighborhood — all soured by a hateful minister — I felt my heart would break.

My deep sorrow led me and my companion to a grove of trees in a park. We poured out our sorrows to the Lord. We cast our burdens on him. The Lord heard our prayers. He helped us feel renewed. We were given special help and were led by the Spirit to new families.

Oh, it's good to laugh off your woes, but sometimes we laugh too much and cry too little. The Lord might smile when we laugh; but when he knows we hurt and we only have him to turn to — he cares. Oh, how he cares! Because, as you know, he loves us dearly.

When engaged in great causes, setbacks must needs be very painful. So feel bad when things don't go well. Don't give up. Go to the Lord.

If you don't hurt at times, you may need to reevaluate your call. There is a time to laugh and a time to cry. May we all be mature enough to know the right time for each.

IMPRESS ME

Write to me each week. Tell me of your successes. When we are together, tell me what is in your heart. Help me to know you. Don't hold back or hide your real feelings from me.

My desire to see you succeed is completely pure. Your success and mine are one. In order to help, I must know you. Don't hold yourself back, striving to not impress me. Go ahead, impress me. Impress me with the fact that you trust me and are willing to talk to me. Impress me with the fact that you love the Lord and have faith in him. Impress me with the fact that you want to repent. Impress me with the fact that you are glad that you are here. Impress me with the fact that you want to be recognized as being capable. Impress me with the fact that you like yourself. Impress me with the fact that you're doing good and want with an intense desire to do better. Impress me with your words. Impress me with your deeds. I love to be impressed. My joy comes when I can say, "You know, you really impress me." After all, to impress someone is to cause him to love you more than he did before. To not want to be impressive is to not want to be a child of God. And the greatest impression you can give is that which comes from being good.

THE GOSPEL WORD

I is a good word. It helps us describe certain things.

Our personal study, personal worthiness, and inner sorrow or joy are all things that can best be described by saying "*I* feel..."; or, "*I* did..."; or, "*I* will..."

We is another equally good word. It's not as personal as *I*, but it's sometimes more powerful.

Missionary teaching or tracting or baptizing can only be accurately described by starting with the word *we*. "*We* did..."; "*We* said..."; "*We* prayed that..."

Sometimes we say, "I told the contact..."; "I decided that we'd..."; "I think I can get him to..."

If that is the way you describe missionary work, you have problems. If that's the way you feel, you will be forever miserable, self-centered, and, in a sense, a failure. When you say "I..." and your companion hears it, he is wounded. Nothing hurts more than helping or trying, and then being cut out of everything by hearing a companion say "I..."

Let's counsel together. Let's seek one another's opinions. Let's know that one personality, no matter how wonderful, cannot be as effective as two. Let's have two testimonies and two prayers. Let's realize that all good ideas don't come from any one head. Let's treat others the way we desire to be treated.

After all, that's the greatest Christlike gift we can give.

MUTUALLY RESPONSIBLE

When I was a missionary, my companion and I were crossing a small footbridge which spanned a river which ran through the city where we labored. Because the bridge was bordered on each side by a high wooden fence and because it turned at an angle just before it ended, it was not possible to see the other side until one turned the corner. Signs were posted, "Do not ride bicycles on the bridge." My companion would put his foot on the pedal, push off with his other foot, and coast. I repeatedly asked him not to do that.

One day, as usual, he did it again. He was about twenty yards ahead of me. He went around the corner and came face to face with an English Bobby (policeman). I arrived on the scene and said, "Officer, if I've told him once, I've told him a hundred times not to do that."

My companion looked at me and seemed to be saying, "Thanks a lot, friend."

The officer, sensing the humor, smiled and said to him: "Now listen carefully, young man. I'm releasing you in the custody of your friend." He then turned to me and said, "From now on you're responsible for him."

I've never forgotten that experience. And, by the way, neither has my companion. I still remind him that he is in my custody. He still reminds me that he really appreciated my thoughtful assistance.

But, you know, that police officer was right. I was responsible for him because he was my companion. And he was responsible for me because I was his. If you save one hundred souls but let your own companion slip further and further away, you're failing instead of succeeding.

If you let him spend his time, hour after hour, doing things unrelated to the proselyting effort, you are failing. If you let him spend undue time visiting members or others just for relaxation, you are failing. If you don't stay with him but let him be alone with girls or women, you are failing. If you let him get by without studying both the scriptures and the discussions on an almost daily basis, you are failing.

If you let him stay in the apartment when you should be out proselyting, you are failing.

We all want to be liked, to be accepted, to be tolerant. But there must be a balance. If we want to become like our Father in heaven, we can't just wink at our companion's weaknesses and let him continue on his way to misery. We must stand up and say: "Elder, I can't do missionary work this way. Let's talk it over. I refuse to be a part of this. I feel our president needs to know what we are doing and unless things change I intend to tell him."

I'm not talking in terms of senior and junior companions. Juniors must help seniors and seniors, juniors. We need to be partners more and leader and follower less. We need to mutually plan and mutually aid one another toward a more excellent way.

We all have weaknesses, so we can't justifiably nag one another. But we also know when someone is really out of line. When we know, we must act. Your companion's mission and perhaps his eternal destiny is in your hands.

As that police officer in England said to me, I say to you, "From now on, you're responsible for him."

COMPANIONS

On my wall is the big chart that holds each of your pictures. To look at the whole board is confusing. It's just a sea of faces. But when my eyes focus upon you — just you — I have a feeling of love sweep through me.

Oh, how often I have wished I could be your companion! We'd really get them — you and I. We'd be the two best average missionaries here. We'd goof off, but only when the time was right. We'd bear testimony to each other. We'd study (but you'd have to help me because I'm not as smart as some). We'd go looking for people each morning. Sometimes we'd feel a little discouraged, but we'd go out anyway. We'd love the members and they'd know it. We'd act in such a way that they'd say, "Don't let the president ever move you two."

We'd teach some great discussions and a few that weren't so great. Sometimes we'd really teach by the Spirit. We'd be good friends with the bishop or branch president. He'd like us a lot. We'd write to each other's parents and encourage them. I'd write to your girl friend.

We'd eat pretty well, especially pancakes. We'd be sort of self-starters. We'd both want to become successful. We'd get a little discouraged if that didn't happen, but we'd keep working hard anyway.

Then one day you'd get transferred. I'd help you pack. You'd tell people good-bye and they'd cry. I'd wonder if people loved me as much as they did you. We'd go the bus. We'd shake hands and I'd feel like crying.

"I'll see you," I'd say. "Remember, we're going to room together at college. And remember at my wedding you'll be my best man." Then you'd go.

I'd go home and wait in the apartment. At 3:45 another bus would come into town. This time another one of you would come into town and we'd start all over. Just you and me — companions.

I love you, my companions. Together we'll be what we ought to be.

REPENTANCE

It's hard to single out one principle that is more important than others. But it seems to me that we (you and me and all of us) need desperately to be able to repent. There's probably no one quite so excited as the person who has repented and knows he's on the right track. I say to you, my fellow companions, there's a lot of forgiveness behind our being here, all of us. And now that we have received a remission of our sins through our repentance and baptism, oh, how important it is to remain clean and pure!

The Doctrine and Covenants (82:7) states, "But unto that soul who sinneth shall the former sins return, saith the Lord your God." In the twentieth section, verse 5, Joseph Smith records, " . . . it was truly manifested unto this first elder that he had received a remission of his sins." This indicates that when Joseph Smith prayed in the grove of trees, one of the things he received was forgiveness of his sins.

I believe there has to be a grove of trees in all our lives, a time when we go before the Lord and lay it all out before him — what we've done and what we intend to do. Often, after having explained it to him, he gives us the impression that we should talk to our priesthood leader. When this is done in the proper manner, when we have a broken heart and a contrite spirit, it's possible for us to receive a remission of our sins.

May the Lord bless us all that we might be able to teach repentance. We've all had some experience with it. The very purpose for our being here is to help each individual repent of his sins. There's no repentance without finally being baptized and receiving the gift of the

Holy Ghost. And there's no place that this can be done except in the Lord's one true church. We are the Lord's agents. This is his church. I bear my humble testimony of that.

SUCCESS

I'm a full-time missionary who is really getting discouraged because baptisms aren't coming. What is "success" when I'm not bringing people into the Church?

Your very question has the ring of success. Your words show that you have such an intense desire to succeed that when it isn't met, it brings sadness to your soul.

We do, and indeed should, measure the success of a mission by the quality and quantity of converts the missionary helps bring into the Church. But that same standard is only a part of the way we measure the success of a man. With this in mind, let us first attempt to measure the success of your mission and then to measure your success as a man. (And of course, when I say *man* I mean woman too.)

If you or I ever decide that the success of a mission doesn't necessarily correlate with the quantity and quality of new converts, then neither of us would make a good missionary. A successful business renders a service or produces something worthwhile, but its overriding success is determined by its profits. An athletic team is successful when it wins. And a mission is a success if it is the means of bringing people into the Church, and that is the real and rather hard truth.

When we keep this idea of success in our minds and work and act and pray accordingly, we are real missionaries. Some say: "We can't make converts here. Not with these people; not now." And thus, through their excuses they begin to feel comfortable. To have such comfort, they pay the price of lowering their goals. Their enthusiasm wanes, and they lose the great edge that is described as the missionary spirit.

Such excuses and decreased aspirations soothe a pain that ought not to be soothed. Instead, all during your mission and throughout your life you should feel disappointed as you recall that your mission was not as successful as you had so deeply desired it would be. Such feelings won't hurt you; as a matter of fact, if properly viewed, they can help you. On the other hand, lower expectations will forever be a stumbling block and will, if repeated in other situations, almost guarantee a life of mediocrity.

Now, let's talk about your success as a man. Be disappointed, my brother, but don't be discouraged. There is a difference, you know. To be discouraged means you are losing courage, and that isn't the case with you. To be disappointed means your goals are not being met, and that's what you are experiencing.

I recall a missionary with whom I talked on a cold winter's day in Kentucky — just he and I alone in a little office. His eyes moistened as he said, "I get the feeling that Mom and Dad wonder why we aren't baptizing anyone." Tears fell as he tried to continue. "They had such high hopes for me, and I'm letting them down. I try, President, I really try; but I just can't seem to do it." I sat silently as he softly cried. Oh, how I loved him! How I hoped that I'd have a son who'd care as much as he cared! You see, I knew him. I knew that when he said he had tried, he really had.

I found myself wishing I could look into his father's eyes and ask: "How did you raise such a son? How did you infuse in him such honor and integrity? How did you teach him to love so completely? How did he come to be so totally responsible?" I could learn many things from the father of such a noble son.

The Spirit of the Lord filled my soul as I sat with him. I knew I was in the presence of a man of God. I told him of my love and respect for him. I told him many things. Then he spoke again: "President, my companion and I will work even harder. I know there's a family waiting for us. We're going to find them and bring them into the Church. You just watch." Days came and went and his full-time mission ended, and he hadn't found the family. But, oh, how he had searched and prayed and worked!

Some time has passed since I last saw him, and I long to see him again. He was one of my most successful missionaries, for he was a real man. As the years roll on, we will meet someday and talk. He will say: "President, I wanted to find a family so much. It broke my heart then and it still does." And then after a thoughtful pause he'll say, "But I sure did try."

I'll look at him with pride and say, "You surely did, you tried with all your heart." And then I'll think, "I hope my own sons will try that hard and be that successful."

Keep being disappointed in your mission until baptisms come. And if some do come, then be disappointed if more don't come. And through all your mission disappointments, conduct yourself in such a way that you'll never be disappointed in yourself. And if that is your lot, then you, my dear friend, will have been and will forever be a successful man.

Book designed by Bailey-Montague and Associates
Composed by Hilton/East and Associates
in Baskerville and Baskerville Medium Italic
Printed by Publishers Press
on 60# Bookcraft Publishers Antique
Bound by Mountain States Bindery
in Kivar 5, Bark Brown Kidskin